HOUSES
OF DEATH

GORDON KERR

canary
press

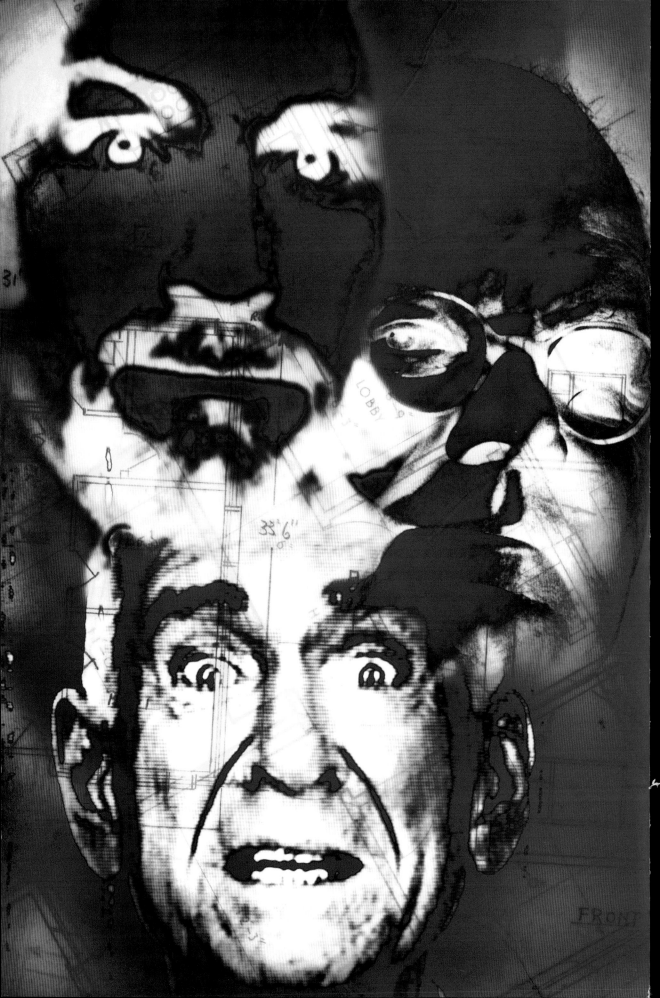

INTRODUCTION

Many of them are no longer there, demolished following the horrific incidents that took place within their walls, as if to expunge them forever. Others have changed their names, often at the request of their occupants, tired of the ghoulish tours and bored with uninvited visitors popping flashbulbs and asking the same old questions. Then there are the houses that are reluctant to let go of their secrets; where the victims and perpetrators of the horrific crimes they hosted still live out the horror that befell them, and can be seen walking the corridors at night or heard screaming endlessly as they relive their terror, again and again. These are the sites of unspeakable, unforgivable and often incomprehensible acts. They are the Houses of Death.

There is no common theme to any of these buildings, although a few of them certainly look the part. The Waverly Hills Sanitorium, for instance, seated on a hill in Louisville, Kentucky, can send a shiver down the spine just from looking at photographs of it. These days its gloomy look is enhanced by dark, dilapidated corridors, rusted pipes and flaking walls. Its sheer size renders it terrifying, but its blood-soaked, death-laden history ensures that this is not a place you would like to visit. Many do, however, seeking ghostly thrills, eager to prove the existence of another world, or simply to be scared out of their wits.

Other buildings in this book were the locations of crimes and atrocities that are almost beyond comprehension. The extermination camps of Nazi Germany were witness to a kind of mass hysteria that resulted in the horrific deaths of millions of Jews, gypsies and other minorities. Perhaps the fact that some of these killing factories, such as Auschwitz, have been allowed to remain as they were, will allow them to serve as a warning to future generations of the horrors that man is sometimes capable of in the service of an ideology.

Of course, from time to time, individuals also commit hideous atrocities that are way beyond the understanding of any sane and rational person. How can we explain the obscene acts perpetrated by Ed Gein on his farm at Plainfield, Wisconsin in the northern United States? A loner, who was fixated by his mother, thrown into a hellish world of peeled human skin and the use of body parts as household items following her death. Of all killers, Gein is one of the hardest to understand. It is a dubious honour he shares with men such as Jeffrey Dahmer and Dennis Nielsen, men who have traversed the boundaries of humanity.

Houses of Death can be ordinary places, too. Dahmer's apartment was just an apartment, although there was always that strange lingering smell about the place. Inside, of course, like Gein's farm and Nielsen's flat, it was a charnel house, but from the outside, there was little evidence of the horror being lived out within. 10 Rillington Place, the venue for John Reginald Christie's macabre, murderous sexual fulfillment, was an unassuming terrace house in the Notting Hill area of north London – in the days before it became the sought-after area to live for film stars and politicians. The house is long gone, replaced by an elevated section of the A40 dual carriageway, but, back then, the innocent passerby would have known little about the obscenities being perpetrated behind that ordinary door.

Then there are the inexplicable tragedies of Jonestown and the Mount Carmel Ranch, settings for the last stands of two messianically deranged individuals, Jim Jones and David Koresh. The bizarre tale of the creation of the Jonestown community, in the middle of the jungle in northwest Guyana, would barely be credible if it was a work of fiction or a film. Incredibly, and tragically for more than 900 people who died there, it was reality of the worst possible kind and the shacks and structures that were witness to the terrible events of 18 November 1978 have now been re-claimed by the jungle; even locals did not want to live there. Mount Carmel, home to the Branch Davidian sect, on the other hand, was obliterated by fire and the scene was bulldozed not long after. The memory lives on, however, of an extraordinary 51-day stand-off, during which this group of buildings filled our TV screens.

Often, it is no more than coincidence which turns an ordinary house into a crime scene – a building simply being the right place, at the right time. Sometimes, however, the very place seems to assume responsibility for the killings carried out inside it. The ruins of Countess Erzsébet Báthory's Castle Csejthe glower down at the visitor, almost daring him or her to enter, and the suffering endured at Philadelphia's Eastern State Penitentiary was caused, in many cases, by the building and its creators, the architects of an inhuman system of punishment and retribution.

CONTENTS

COUNTESS
ERZSEBET
BATHORY
CASTLE CSEJTHE, SLOVAKIA

COUNTESS ERZEBET BATHORY WAS A TRULY EVIL WOMAN, BUT HER ROYAL CONNECTIONS ENSURED HER PROTECTION, EVEN WHEN THE NUMEROUS HIDEOUS CRIMES SHE HAD COMMITTED WERE FINALLY REVEALED. WHILE HER ACCOMPLICES WERE TORTURED AND EXECUTED, THE COUNTESS WAS IMPRISONED IN HER CASTLE HOME AND SIMPLY LEFT TO DIE A NATURAL, IF NOT PEACEFUL, DEATH.

Villages would wait in dread. In the dead of night, the carriage, drawn by powerful black stallions, would drive noisily past. Inside would be young girls, cowering in fear. They had every right to be afraid. They would enter the huge Castle Csejthe and never be seen again. People living nearby reported hearing horrific screams emanating from behind the castle walls. There was talk of witchcraft, orgies and vile practices.

Nothing could be done about it, however. The beautiful denizen of the castle, Countess Erzsébet Báthory, was as well connected as they came. Her family included counts, princes, bishops and cardinals. She was a cousin of the prime minister, her uncle, Stephen, had been king of Poland and she had once been married to the warrior count known to Hungarians as the 'Black Hero' because of the courage he showed in battles against the hated Turks.

Eventually, however, King Mathias II of Hungary decided that it was time to bring an end to the rumours that had been spreading about the countess. Either that, or bring an end to what was going on behind the forbidding walls of the castle. He sent a party to investigate, a party that included her cousin, the prime minister. They had to be careful, but, in all likelihood, on seeing her cousin's colours, she would open the castle's massive gates to them.

The party was surprised to find the door of the castle open when they arrived, and they entered a great hall. Immediately, they found a young, partly clothed girl lying on the floor. She was unnaturally pale, as if the blood had been drained out of her body. She was dead, and another girl they found nearby was close to death. She, too, looked as if the blood had been sucked from her body, and the many piercings that peppered her body seemed to confirm that fact. Further on, a woman was found chained to a post. She had been whipped and her body was lacerated and burned. Like the others, her blood appeared to have been taken.

In the dungeons, they discovered cells filled with women and children who had been beaten and abused. They released them and escorted them from the castle, before returning to continue their grim search.

Countess Erzsébet Báthory had married at fifteen. Count Ferencz Nádasdy, her husband, was a warrior and rarely at home, giving Erzsébet ample opportunity to indulge in unsavoury pastimes. That was not unusual in her family, though. Her aunt was reputed to be a witch, she had an uncle who was an alchemist and a devil-worshipper and her brother was a paedophile. Her nurse was said to be a practitioner of black magic and was reputed to have been involved in the sacrifice of children.

As if that was not bad enough, her husband had a number of unsavoury habits, many of which he passed on to his young wife. He was partial to beating servant girls to within an inch of their lives or spreading honey on their naked bodies and tying them down in the open, leaving them to be bitten and stung by insects. When he was not doing that, he was freezing girls to death by pouring water over their naked bodies in the icy depths of winter and leaving them to die. His idea of a love token to his wife was a black magic spell from whichever land he was fighting in. While he was gone, she also took countless lovers, both male and female. However, the count died in 1604, leaving Erzsébet a widow at 44, with four young children.

She returned to her estates after a spell in Vienna, and it was at this point that pretty young women began to disappear from neighbouring villages. The girls were promised that they were going to be taken into service at the castle, but, once there, they were subjected to horrific treatment, locked up in cellars, beaten and tortured, often by Erzsébet, herself. Their bodies were then cut up with razors and burned.

Erzsébet was known to sew servants' mouths shut or force them to eat pieces of their own flesh or burn their genitals. When she was ill and could not indulge in these horrors, she would attempt to bite those who approached her bed, like a wild animal.

From peasant girls, she shifted her attention to girls of noble families, confident that no one would try to stop her. She offered to teach social graces to them, but when they arrived at Castle Csejthe, she tortured and killed them, as she had done the peasant girls. This was a step too far and, like many psychopaths, she had mistakenly begun to think she was invincible. Following the murder of one young woman, whose death she had tried to make look like suicide, the king decided enough was enough.

The investigating party found bones and human remains, as well as clothing belonging to the missing girls. There were bodies everywhere, their arms and eyes missing. Some had been burned or partially burned, and many had been buried in shallow graves around the castle. Dogs ran about with body-parts in their mouths.

Erzsébet did not attend her trial which began on 2 January, 1611. Countless witnesses testified, many of whom had suffered at her hands in Castle Csejthe. However, it was her accomplices who provided the most damning testimony. Ficzko, a dwarf who worked for Erzsébet, testified that he was uncertain how many women he helped to kill, but he did know that 37 girls had been murdered. A nurse, Ilona Joo, confessed to killing about 50. She described how she pushed red-hot pokers into victims' mouths or up their noses. She described how her mistress had placed her fingers in the mouth of one girl and pulled hard until the sides split open. Victims were forced to indulge in deviant sexual practices and one was made to strip flesh off her own arm.

The countess and her accomplices were convicted of 80 counts of murder, although it is thought that there may have been as many as 300 victims.

While her accomplices were gruesomely tortured and killed – fingers pulled off, buried alive or beheaded – the countess was imprisoned for life, proclaiming her innocence throughout. She died in either 1613 or 1614.

It was later claimed that she killed her victims and stole their blood in order to bathe in it. She believed it made her look younger.

EASTERN STATE PENITENTIARY

PHILADELPHIA, PENNSYLVANIA, USA

TODAY, EASTERN STATE PENITENTIARY LIES EMPTY, APART FROM THRILL-SEEKING TOURISTS ACCOMPANIED BY TOUR GUIDES, AND THE OCCASIONAL TV CREW. BUT ESP WAS ONCE HOME TO SOME OF AMERICA'S MOST DANGEROUS CRIMINALS – MEN AND WOMEN WHOSE ALREADY UNSTABLE MINDS WERE ROUTINELY PUSHED TO THE LIMIT BY THE PRISON'S BRUTAL REGIME.

In most prisons, solitary confinement was a punishment. In Eastern State Penitentiary, in Philadelphia, it was the norm.

Eastern State was devised by Philadelphia's Quakers, for whom the concept of penitence was very important. They considered the brutal regimes of correctional institutions up to that time to have been unsuccessful, and believed there was another way to deal with criminals. They invented the 'Philadelphia System' of imprisonment that encouraged solitary confinement as the means of rehabilitation, and put it into practice in Eastern State Penitentiary.

The prison was designed by one of the city's most successful architects, John Haviland, who created a building based on a 'hub and spoke' design, seven cell blocks radiating out from the central guard post. Its design allowed constant supervision from a central rotunda. It was considered so successful that it was borrowed by more than 300 penal institutions across the world. It opened its doors to 250 prisoners in 1829, but was only finally completed in 1836.

A prisoner entering the prison was stripped of his clothing and given a medical. He was allocated a number and would not hear his name spoken for the duration of his imprisonment. He was given a pair of woollen trousers, a jacket with his number sewn on it, two handkerchiefs, two pairs of socks and a pair of shoes. A hood made of rough cloth was then put over his head and he was led to his cell. It was thought prisoners would find it harder to escape if they were unfamiliar with the route to the cells. Cell doors were so small that prisoners had to stoop to enter – it made it more difficult to attack the warders and also, according to the Quakers, reminded them of the humility they should be feeling. In the cell, the only light came from a slit high up in the ceiling, known as 'the eye of God'. It was designed to make feel as if they were being watched by the supreme being at all times.

Cells were small and prisoners spent most of their day locked up. Unusually, for those days, when most houses lacked facilities, each cell had running water and a toilet and a basin. However, this was merely another means of ensuring that they would not meet and communicate with fellow prisoners. They were provided with a Bible, a table and a bunk and were locked in their cells 23 hours a day. The other hour was spent exercising in the exercise yard, surrounded by high walls, that were attached to each individual cell. Prisoners, desperate for human communication, threw notes, wrapped around stones, over the walls into their neighbour's exercise yard. Or, they would tap gently on the pipes that ran through the prison or whisper through air vents.

The most noticeable thing at Eastern State was the deadening silence, a silence that drove many inmates out of their minds. It had to be observed at all times. Guards even wore socks over their shoes to cut down noise, and inmates were not allowed to make a sound – no singing or whistling or even talking to themselves. If they breached this, the prison's most important rule, they were severely punished.

Punishment was mild in the beginning, in comparison to other prisons, but as time wore on, the prison authorities began to devise harsher penalties for rule-breakers.

The 'water bath' involved being dipped into a bath of ice-cold water and then hung on a wall for the night. Often the water on the prisoner's skin would form into a layer of ice by morning. The 'mad chair' was a particularly harsh punishment that had been adopted from the 'treatment' of the mentally ill in asylums. Ironically it often drove victims insane before they were released. Prisoners were strapped so tightly into a chair that they could not make even the slightest movement, sometimes being left for days. The limbs would become stiff and swollen as the circulation was cut off and would then turn a bluish-black colour.

The 'iron gag' was the most feared of all the punishments. The prisoner's arms were tied behind his neck and a gag was attached to his tongue and his hands. The slightest movement tore at the gag, ripping the prisoner's tongue and causing intense pain.

The 'hole' was a pit, dug under the cellblock, reserved for the most difficult of inmates. They were kept there sometimes for weeks, receiving only a daily ration of one cup of water and one slice of bread.

Although disease was rife at Eastern State, insanity rapidly became the most common illness. It became so common that doctors invented causes, the most popular of which was excessive masturbation. If it was not masturbation, it was put down to their genes. Of course, it was horrific isolation that was the real cause.

Eastern State became the most famous prison in the world and had many visitors, not all of whom were impressed by what they were shown. English writer, Charles Dickens, was horrified when he was given a tour in 1845. 'The system here is rigid, strict and hopeless solitary confinement I believe it, in its effects, to be cruel and wrong,' he wrote. He went on to describe it as a 'torturing of the mind that is much worse that any physical punishment that can be administered'.

Escape attempts were generally unsuccessful. In 1926, one group dug a tunnel 10.5 m (35 ft) long before being caught. In 1945, another group dug a tunnel that extended beyond the wall. They were apprehended a few blocks away from the prison. In 1932, William Hamilton was serving dinner in the warden's apartment. When the warden left him alone for a few minutes, Hamilton tied together some bed sheets and climbed out of the window. He was not recaptured until 1937, when he was returned to the same cell he had left five years previously.

Solitary confinement was finally abandoned in the 1870s, and Eastern State became an ordinary prison. It was reformed in 1913, when its numbers had risen to 1,700 and it had become dangerously overcrowded. By 1970, it was in a state of disrepair, and it was decided it would be too expensive to renovate it yet again. It was abandoned and became a National Historic Monument, used in films such as *Twelve Monkeys* and TV ghost-hunting programmes. It lies empty now, apart from the many ghosts, which are said to wander its crumbling corridors.

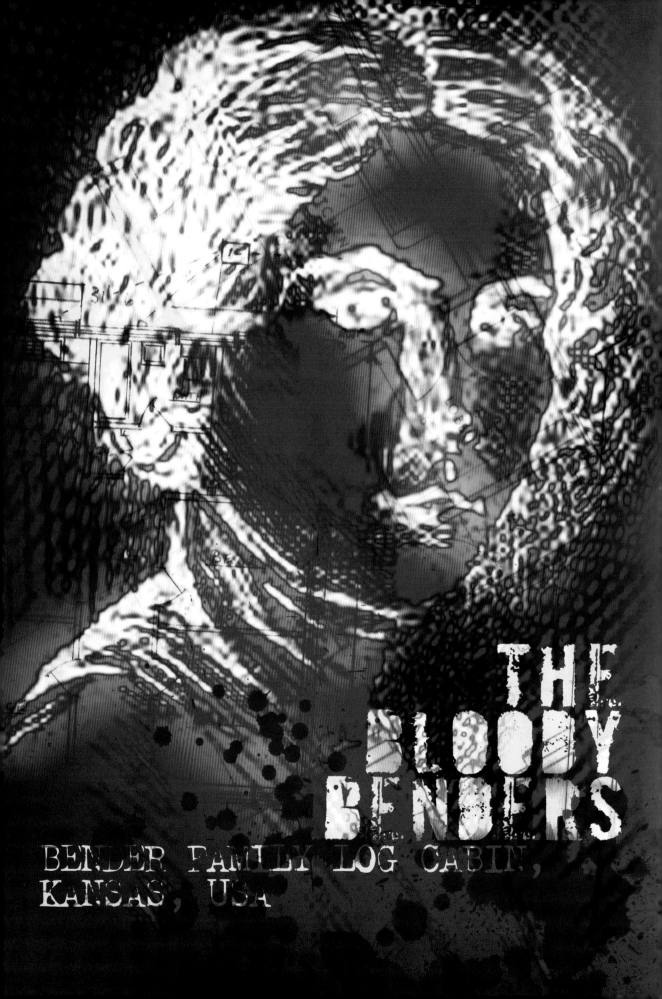

THE
BLOODY
BENDERS

BENDER FAMILY LOG CABIN,
KANSAS, USA

WHEN POLICE AND SOUVENIR-HUNTERS
FINALLY FINISHED DECIMATING THE
SITE OF THE INFAMOUS BENDERS' LOG
CABIN, ALL THAT REMAINED WAS A
HOLE IN THE GROUND THAT WAS ONCE
THE CELLAR. THE CABIN ITSELF AND
THE OUTBUILDINGS HAD GONE, BUT,
ACCORDING TO LOCALS, GHOSTS OF THE
BENDERS' MANY UNFORTUNATE VICTIMS
CONTINUED TO HAUNT THE AREA.

She was around eight years of age and the report in the *Kansas City Times* recorded the discovery of her body: 'The little girl had long, sunny hair and some traces of beauty on a countenance that was not yet entirely disfigured by decay. One arm was broken. The breastbone had been driven in. The right knee had been wrenched from its socket and the leg doubled up under the body.' Most gruesome of all was the discovery that none of her wounds had been serious enough to kill her, meaning only one thing; she had been buried alive. And she was not the only horribly disfigured body they uncovered during those grisly few days.

The Bender family had come to Kansas, like many other pioneers, after the ousting of the Osage Indians from south-east Kansas freed up large swathes of land for homesteaders. Consisting of John Bender Sr, his wife – Ma Bender, son John Jr and daughter Kate. The Bender family were part of a large group of 'spiritualist' families that settled in western Labette County. Sixty-year-old John Sr settled his family on a 65 hectare (160 acre) plot that was handily positioned on the important and busy Osage-Mission Independence Trail. They constructed a small, one-roomed cabin, partitioned by a large piece of canvas into living quarters at the back and a store at the front where they sold a few essentials and served meals to hungry travellers.

John Bender Sr was a bear of a man with a huge beard and deep-set eyes. Mrs Bender, an unfriendly woman, with an impenetrably guttural accent like her husband, claimed she was a medium and that she could converse with the dead. She also claimed to be able to cast spells. Daughter Kate's English was as good and she was a handsome, auburn-haired 23 year-old who, like her mother, claimed to possess psychic powers. She distributed leaflets advertizing her skills at curing illnesses and gave lectures about spiritualism.

Travellers on the Mission-Independence Trail were seeking to establish a new life for themselves out west and, consequently, often carried large sums of money to buy land. It was noticed that a number of them were disappearing. They seemed to reach the Big Hill Country of south-eastern Kansas and simply vanish.

Of course, these were wild times and communications were far from good, but, even so, people began to worry and wary travellers began to avoid that part of the trail.

Ten people were known to have disappeared, including a well-known doctor from Independence, William H York, who had set out to investigate the mysterious disappearance of a father and his daughter. They had left Independence en route for Iowa in the winter of 1872, but had simply vanished from the face of the earth. Dr York began his search in spring 1873, stopping at numerous homesteads to make enquiries. However, his search had proven fruitless and he was preparing to return to Independence on 8 March. He never arrived home.

The locals were also becoming worried and a meeting was convened to discuss the disappearances. Shortly after this, however, a passing neighbour noticed that the Bender homestead looked deserted. Indeed, the animals had not been fed and the cabin had been stripped of anything useful. It looked, in fact, as if the family had left in a hurry. Furthermore, there was a disgusting smell in the air.

A trapdoor in the cabin floor was discovered, leading to a 1.8 m (6 ft) deep hole in which was found clotted blood, the source of the stench. Locals began to dig the earth under the cabin, having moved the entire structure to one side in order to do so. However, they found nothing. They then began to investigate the land around the cabin, where they had more success.

The first body was that of Dr York, who had been buried face down after his skull had been smashed and his throat cut. It did not end there. The next day, nine more bodies were dug up, including a woman and the little girl, and body parts were also found.

Rewards were offered for the capture of the 'Bloody' Benders, as they became known. Dr York's brother put up $1,000 (£500.00) and the Governor of Kansas, Thomas Osborn, offered $2,000 (£1000). Meanwhile, the sensational news of the murders spread like wildfire and thousands turned up at the Bender Cabin, including newspaper reporters from all over America.

It was not even as if the Benders had gained great riches from their horrific acts. In fact, it was estimated that the most they had been able to steal from their victims was around $4,600 (£2,300), a few horses, a pony, a couple of wagons and a saddle. Some of the people they killed had nothing at all to offer. Therefore, where motive was concerned, it could only be assumed that they had killed their victims for the sheer thrill of it.

Some men managed to escape and they came forward with their stories. One told how Kate had threatened him with a knife after he had refused to sit with his back to the curtain because of the disgusting, and frankly suspicious, stains that covered it. He fled, as had a Catholic priest who spotted one of the Bender men hiding a hammer.

A manhunt was launched and the Benders were found to have boarded a train to the town of Humboldt. At Chanute, however, John Jr and Kate changed trains, heading for Dennison in Texas. Meanwhile, John Sr and Ma Bender were thought to have headed for St. Louis.

There were sightings of Ma Bender and Kate for years and, in 1889, two women resembling them were arrested in Detroit and extradited to Kansas. The case against them was eventually dropped, however, due to lack of evidence.

The truth about the family's real identities emerged only later. John Bender Sr. was actually John Flickinger, who had originated from either Germany or Holland. It was reported that he had committed suicide in Lake Michigan in 1884. There were those who claimed, however, that he had actually been killed by his wife and daughter after running off with their ill-gotten gains.

Mrs Bender is thought to have been born Almira Meik in the Adirondack Mountains in northern New York State. She had had a series of husbands and several children, all of who died suspiciously, perhaps as a result of a blow with a hammer.

John Jr turned out not to have been related to any of them. His real name was John Gebhardt, and it emerged that he was involved in a relationship with Kate who was not, after all, his sister. It is said that whenever she became pregnant with his child, she would give birth and then kill the baby with the family's murder implement of choice – a hammer.

BELOW: As locals unearth body after body, people from all over the region gather at the Bender property.

SING SING
OSSINING, NEW YORK, USA

THE NAME 'SING SING' IS THOUGHT TO BE DERIVED FROM THE NATIVE AMERICAN PHRASE 'SINT SINCK', WHICH TRANSLATES AS 'STONE UPON STONE'. SING SING CORRECTIONAL FACILITY WAS ORIGINALLY NAMED 'MOUNT PLEASANT' WHEN IT OPENED IN 1828, BUT LIFE AT THE PRISON WAS ANYTHING BUT.

The state of New York has executed more people in the past 75 years than any other state in America – probably more than 600 – and the centre for those executions has been Sing Sing Correctional Facility, a maximum-security prison in Ossining, some 48km (30 miles) north of New York City. The prison was constructed near a village also bearing the name Sing Sing, derived from the Indian 'Sint Sinks', that translates as 'stone upon stone'.

The New York executioner's job is a demanding one, and not just because so many inhabitants of the great city commit capital crimes. He is also executioner for Massachusetts, New Jersey and Connecticut, sometimes dispatching convicted criminals in more than one state in the space of a day.

Edwin Davis was Sing Sing's first executioner, at a time when the executioner enjoyed the euphemistic job title of 'electrician'. Davis was in charge when the

first criminal to occupy the electric chair, William Kemmler, was executed at Auburn Prison, in August 1890. Kemmler had got drunk and killed his girlfriend with an axe, but the execution went badly. After the current was switched off, Kemmler was still very much alive, and a number of witnesses fainted. Another 2,000 volts were shot into his body, rupturing blood vessels under his skin and setting his body on fire. In all, the execution took eight minutes, and one observer commented, 'They would have done better using an axe.'

In the 19th century, many executions took place in New York on Bedloe's Island, better known now as the Statue of Liberty. But once the decision had been taken to establish Sing Sing as the execution site for New York, a new death house had to be built. It cost a staggering amount for the time, $268,000 (£134,000). Separate from the main prison buildings, it was entirely self-sufficient with its own kitchen, hospital

OPPOSITE PAGE: The electric chair at Sing Sing Prison, circa 1950.

BELOW: The execution of convicted murderer, William Kemmler, the first man to die in the electric chair. Three surges of electricity were needed to finish the job.

HE EXECUTED SEVEN MEN IN LESS THAN AN HOUR

and a room for carrying out autopsies. It was ready by 1917 and, from then on, New York's unfortunate condemned were sent to what became known as the 'Big House' to prepare to meet their maker.

It was there that Davis carried out Sing Sing's first execution by electricity in July 1891. Harris A Smiler was followed in rapid succession by three other condemned men in the newly installed electric chair. But multiple executions were not uncommon, and on 12 August 1912, he executed seven men in less than an hour at Sing Sing. He also executed Martha Place, the first woman electrocuted in America, in 1899.

John Hilbert took over when Davis eventually retired, in 1914, and executed 140 people in New York, Massachusetts and Kansas. However, Hilbert's mental well-being was damaged by the job and he suffered from depression. Once, he fainted half an hour before he was due to execute two men. Hilbert retired abruptly, just before an execution in 1926, and was replaced by 52-year-old Robert G Elliot. Tragically, Hilbert shot himself.

Robert Elliot was a pragmatic individual, and he approached his work as just a job that someone had to do. 'I'm just an ordinary human being,' he once said, 'I'm no more responsible for killing these men than the judge or jury.' Nonetheless, he was a victim of press stories suggesting he was something of a social outcast and a recluse. Among the 387 men and women he executed, until he retired through ill health in 1939, were a number of infamous criminals – Sacco and Vanzetti and Bruno Hauptman, killer of the Lindbergh baby, among them.

The remainder of Sing Sing prison was not exactly paradise on earth. It had been commissioned in 1825 when an upstate New York prison warder, captain Elam Lynds, was given the job of finding a location for a new prison and building it. He embarked upon the construction using 100 inmates from Auburn prison, who built the prison from scratch in desperate conditions.

The design was for 800 cells, stacked one on top of the other, four cells high in a

ABOVE: The interior of Sing Sing Prison, circa 1935.

OPPOSITE PAGE: Bernard Richard Hauptman, arrested in New York for conspiracy to kidnap a young boy, September 29th 1934.

building 145m (476 ft) long. The cells were tiny – 2.1m (7ft) long by 1m (3ft) wide and 1.98m (6ft 7ins) high. The building was completed in 1828.

The system utilized at Sing Sing was similar to that in a number of other US prisons. Lynds had himself encapsulated it when working at Auburn, where the silent regime was invented. 'The [prisoners] are not to exchange a word with each other under any pretence whatever; not to communicate in writing. They must not sing, whistle, dance, run, jump, or do anything that has a tendency in the least degree to disturb the harmony or regulations of the prison,' he wrote.

What they were allowed to do, however, was work, and prisons contracted out labour to private companies. At Sing Sing, they made furniture, carpets, tapestry, shoes, bedding, cigars and cut stone, working ten hours a day. Of course, the money earned mostly went back into prison funds, but large amounts also bolstered the incomes of prison warders.

Punishment was brutal and regular at Sing Sing. In 1864, it is reported, of

796 inmates, 613 received some form of physical punishment. These punishments were cruel in the extreme. One of the worst was 'The Bath', which was used for decades. The miscreant was tied to a chair and a shield was attached to his head that allowed water to rise up over his chin and mouth. The water could be dropped from a great height onto the prisoner's head. Solitary confinement was also regularly dished out, as was the punishment of being 'bucked'. In this, a wooden bar was inserted between a prisoner's arms and legs while he was seated. The bar was then hoisted onto a stand and the prisoner was left hanging upside down.

Beating and flogging were common. One inmate described a lashing he had witnessed in the prison yard in the middle of the 19th century. The victim was lashed 133 times, the skin on his back being shredded by the whip. When he complained, the guard approached him and dealt him a blow across the mouth with his cane, ordering him to be quiet.

Food was scarce and poor – inmates received two eggs a year. In this atmosphere of despair and hopelessness, suicide was common. Being sent 'up the river', as a trip to Sing Sing was called, usually meant you would not be making a return journey.

Around 1900, there were a number of changes at Sing Sing. The hated lockstep where prisoners had to walk in line close together, was abandoned, as was the striped uniform. More windows were installed and inmates were given greater access to the exercise yard. However, Sing Sing was in a bad way, and it was not until the arrival of an enlightened warder from upstate New York, Lewis E Lawes, in 1919, that things improved.

Lawes found a prison in a state of chaos, suffering from decades of abuse and neglect. Money was missing from the prison bank account and there were even prisoners missing. A head count of male prisoners came up with only 762, when there should have been 795. Of the 102 female prisoners who should have been there, he counted only 82. There was no record whatsoever of one prisoner's admission or stay. It was decided he must have been a volunteer, and he was released.

Lawes began a campaign of modernization with new buildings, a chapel, a library and a mess hall.

In 1943, the old cellblock was finally closed. It had been home and place of death to some of America's most notorious villains – Louis 'Lepke' Buchalter, the head of Murder Inc.; Charles Becker, the first American policeman executed for murder; Albert Fish, serial killer and cannibal; Charles Chapin, ('The Rose Man'), a former New York City newspaper editor, who served life for murder; Ethel and Julius Rosenberg, executed for spying for the Soviet Union; Martha Beck and Raymond Fernandez, electrocuted there for the murders of 12 people; Willie Sutton, the bank robber; Carl Panzram, the prolific serial killer; George C. Parker, the con artist who sold the Brooklyn Bridge; Frank Abbandando, former member of Murder Inc. and Louis Capone, former member of Murder Inc.

LIZZIE BORDEN

92 SECOND STREET,
FALL RIVER, MASSACHUSETTS, USA

TODAY, 92 SECOND STREET, FALL RIVER, IS A WELL-KNOWN FIRST-CLASS BED AND BREAKFAST OWNED BY LEE-ANN WILBUR AND DONALD WOODS. THE COUPLE HAVE TURNED THEIR PROPERTY INTO A MUSEUM, ENCOURAGING VISITORS TO EXPLORE THE BORDEN FAMILY MURDERS AND FORM THEIR OWN OPINIONS ABOUT THE GUILT OR INNOCENCE OF PRIME-SUSPECT AND FOLK LEGEND: LIZZIE BORDEN.

AJ Borden's body lay on its right side on the sofa, where he had sat down to have a nap after coming home from work. His feet still rested on the floor and his head lay inclined to the right. His face had received 11 blows from something sharp and heavy. It was not a pretty sight. One eye had been cut in half and hung out of its socket and his nose had been sliced off. There was blood everywhere – on the sofa, on the floor and dripping from a picture on the wall.

Upstairs, in a bedroom, they discovered AJ's wife, Abbey. She had been dealt 19 blows from behind that had crushed her skull. She was covered in congealed blood.

It was the morning of 4 August 1892, a swelteringly hot day in Fall River, Massachusetts, and the only people present in the house at the time of the murders were AJ's daughter, Lizzie – Abbey was her stepmother – and a servant, Bridget Sullivan.

It had been a normal morning for seventy-year-old Andrew J Borden. He had gone to the bank and the post office before returning home. AJ, as he was known, was one of the richest men in Fall River. Tall, thin and white-haired, he was also one of the most unpopular men in town, renowned for his thrift. He was too mean, for instance, to install indoor plumbing and, in the undertakers he owned, was rumoured to cut the feet off corpses so that they would fit into smaller and, consequently, cheaper coffins.

His meanness had almost tragic results several days before his murder. The entire family was laid low with chronic food poisoning, but, according to some reports, it was caused by the fact that the meat they had eaten had been kept in a broken freezer that he was too mean to have repaired. Of course, there were also those who claimed that Lizzie had tried to poison them all. Nonetheless, when a doctor called at the house to treat them, stingy old AJ sent him packing, refusing even to pay for a house call.

The gruesome murders of AJ and Abbey Borden became a national sensation and a full-blown media frenzy ensued. The reason for the media's interest was the mystery and conjecture that surrounded the killings. There was no murder weapon, although an axe was found in a woodshed that was claimed to have been used, even though it was clean. The handle was broken off and the prosecution claimed it had been broken and disposed of because it had been soaked in blood. However, as seemed to be a regular feature of this case, there was disagreement – one police officer claimed the broken part of the handle was lying beside it and another claimed that it wasn't.

There was conjecture, too, about the blood. Such vicious and bloody attacks would lead one to expect the murderer's clothes to be covered in blood. So, where were they, especially if one of the two women present in the house at the time, Lizzie and the servant, Bridget, was the killer? There was a report of Lizzie burning a light-blue dress in the stove, but she claimed it had been stained with whitewash. However, no one could even agree on what colour dress she had been wearing on the day. Another story has Bridget Sullivan carrying a bundle out of the house, but, again, there was no evidence to support this.

Lizzie and Bridget both told police their movements at the time that the crime was committed. Bridget had been instructed by Abbey Borden to clean all the windows in the house, but Lizzie changed her story several times. She initially said she had been in her room and then said she had been in the basement. Finally, she claimed to have gone out to the barn where she had remained for 40 minutes. This was thought to be slightly odd, as it was 38°C (100°F) outside and would have been even hotter in the barn.

Life at 92 Second Street had become increasingly unpleasant of late. Relations between parents and children were so bad that they had virtually split the house in two, Lizzie and Emma occupying the front part of the house and the parents the rear.

The cause of much of the argument was AJ's will. He had already given a house to Abbey's relatives and the girls' uncle had come to visit that week in order to organize the transfer of farm property, including a summer house that the girls loved. Shortly before the murders, both girls had briefly left home on what were termed 'extended vacations', but Lizzie had decided to return early.

Eventually, the police decided to arrest Lizzie Borden and charge her with the two murders. However, after only an hour's deliberation, the jury found her not guilty. There was just not enough evidence to convict her.

Speculation continues as to who killed the Bordens. An axe murder in the same area, not long after Lizzie's acquittal, helped her cause, but there is still disagreement.

Bridget Sullivan returned to her native Ireland, returning to live and eventually die in Butte, Montana, in 1948 and, although ostracized by her neighbours ever after, Lizzie Borden continued to live in Fall River until her eventual death, in 1927, aged 66. Her name continues to echo down the years, especially in the popular children's skipping rhyme:

Lizzie Borden took an axe
And gave her mother forty whacks.
And when she saw what she had done
She gave her father forty-one.

HH HOLMES

THE MURDER CASTLE, CHICAGO, USA

THE CASTLE STANDS OUT AMONG
OTHER HOUSES OF DEATH BECAUSE
IT WAS DESIGNED AND BUILT WITH
KILLING IN MIND. PSYCHOPATH, HH
HOLMES, DEDICATED HIS LIFE TO TWO
THINGS: GRUESOME MURDERS AND
THE PURSUIT OF MONEY. IT IS IMPOSSIBLE
TO SAY WHICH ONE HE LOVED MORE,
BUT THE CHICAGO WORLD FAIR
OFFERED HIM THE PERFECT
OPPORTUNITY TO DELIGHT IN
BOTH HIS FAVOURITE PASTIMES.

Holmes called it his 'Castle'.

It was built on three stories and boasted 100 rooms. With soundproof sleeping chambers, complete with peepholes; asbestos-padded walls; gas pipes; walls that slid across, making a room bigger or smaller, as necessary, and trapdoors with ladders leading down to the rooms below. It was a maze of secret passages and false doors, and a number of the rooms were filled with gruesome torture equipment. Chillingly, there was also a specially equipped surgery. Holmes is thought to have placed his victims in special rooms into which he pumped lethal gas, watching their death throes through peepholes. On occasion, he might even set fire to the gas in order to add a little more excitement. When he tired of that, there was always the 'elasticity determinator', an elongated bed to which a victim was tightly strapped and then stretched. Holmes liked to experiment. Chutes, the sides greased for easier dispatch, led down to a two-level basement with a large furnace burning fiercely. Once he had finished with a corpse, it slid down a chute to the basement where he used vats of acid and other chemicals to get rid of any evidence that it had ever existed. Alternatively, he might remove all the flesh and sell the skeleton to a local medical school.

HH Holmes – real name Hermann Webster Mudgett – arrived in Chicago in the 1880s. The city was brimming with excitement as well as visitors, as the World's Fair, or Great Exposition, was about to take place. The hordes of people – some estimates put it at a staggering 27 million – passing through the city, put a strain on the forces of law and order, but also opened up opportunities for crime and for psychopaths, such as Mudgett, now going under the name Holmes. He found work as a prescription clerk in a pharmacy when he first came to town, but the owner of the premises where he worked left town suddenly, or 'went to California' as Holmes said at the time. She and her daughter were never heard of again, and it is almost certain that he killed them. He took

OPPOSITE PAGE: A diagram depicting a floor plan of HH Holmes's 'murder castle', as originally featured in the *Chicago Tribune*.

ownership of the business and bought an empty property across the road, on 63rd Street.

He began to raise money through murder and fraud in order to build his 'Castle', and then let rooms to young women who had come to Chicago to enjoy the fair. Of course, they quickly disappeared, as did a number of the women he employed. They were forced to take out life-insurance policies as a condition of their employment, and he claimed on these as he dispatched the women. He also carried out hundreds of illegal abortions in the Castle's dark rooms, many of his patients did not survive the procedure.

When investigators finally examined the Castle, after Holmes's arrest, the media had a field day. 'The Castle is a Tomb!' screamed the headline in the *Chicago Tribune*. The *Philadelphia Inquirer* called it a 'charnel house'. True crime writers quickly made it a staple of the genre. In Philadelphia, a Holmes Museum opened. As for the narcissistic Holmes, he wrote a memoir, *Holmes' Own Story, in which the Alleged Multimurderer and Arch Conspirator Tells of the Twenty-two Tragic Deaths and Disappearances in which he is Said to be Implicated*. 'My sole object in this publication is to vindicate my name from the horrible aspersions cast upon it,' he wrote, 'and to appeal to a fair-minded American public for a suspension of judgment.'

In the book, Holmes describes the day that his unhealthy interest in medical matters began. A gang of boys tried to frighten him by confronting him with a skeleton in a local doctor's office. Rather than terrify him, it made him resolve to pursue a career in medicine. His first job was in an asylum, an experience that scarred him. He then moved to Chicago.

Holmes's finances were in a mess at the end of the World's Fair, and, with creditors moving in, he abandoned Chicago and moved to Fort Worth, Texas. He had killed a couple of railroad heiress sisters, but, before killing them, had arranged their affairs so that he would inherit property they owned in Texas. He intended to construct another death factory, along the lines of the Castle in Chicago, but the authorities in Texas were not as easily fooled as those in Chicago and he abandoned the project.

He set off on travels around the US and Canada, and is thought, in all likelihood, to have continued in his murderous ways, although no bodies were found to corroborate this.

It was Holmes's killing of his business partner, Benjamin Pitezel, and his children, that was his downfall. Pitezel and Holmes had concocted a scheme whereby Pitezel would fake his death so that his wife could collect on a $10,000 (£20,000) insurance policy. This would be split with Holmes, whose role in the scheme was to provide a body to stand in for Pitezel. But Holmes, who never really liked Pitezel, actually did kill him and used the real corpse to collect the insurance money. He told Mrs Pitezel that her husband was hiding out in South America and persuaded her to allow him to have custody of three of her five children. The three children were killed in various locations as he travelled across America.

But Holmes's luck was finally running out. Pinkerton's Detective Agency had been on his heels for a while, and they finally arrested him in Boston, in November 1894. They had long had suspicions about his activities, but it was only when they gained entry to the Castle, that these suspicions were confirmed.

Holmes confessed to 27 murders, although it is believed he may have murdered as many as 230 people. On 17 May 1896, he was hanged in Philadelphia and was buried, at his own request, in cement, so that his body could not be dug up and dissected. It was a pity, many thought, that he denied such a right to his many victims.

By the time he died, the Castle was no more. On 19 August 1895, the building was destroyed by a mysterious fire. A US post office now occupies the site of the killing factory run by America's first infamous serial killer.

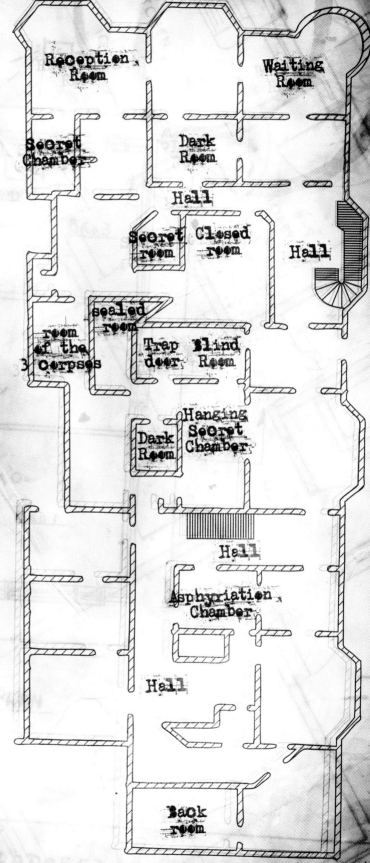

NEWGATE PRISON

CITY OF LONDON, ENGLAND

THE STENCH WAS UNIMAGINABLE, AND PERMEATED THE AIR AROUND NEWGATE TO SUCH AN EXTENT THAT SHOPS AROUND IT HAD TO CLOSE DURING THE WARM SUMMER MONTHS. GAOL FEVER WAS RIFE, EXACERBATED BY THE ROTTING CADAVERS LITTERING THE CORRIDORS AND THE DISEASE-RIDDEN RATS AND LICE. IN THE WORDS OF SIR STEPHEN JANSEN, NEWGATE PRISON WAS AN 'ABOMINABLE SINK OF BEASTLINESS AND CORRUPTION'.

Of the 150 prisons in London during the 18th century, Newgate Prison was probably the one to which one least wanted to be sent. It was the largest, most notorious and, undoubtedly, the worst of those filthy, rat-infested institutions. In fact, Newgate was so bad that only a quarter of condemned prisoners actually survived until execution day – a small mercy.

There had been a prison on its site since the 12th century, and had it been demolished and re-built many times in its 700-year history.

Three hundred years ago, prisons were privately run and it was a lucrative job being a jailer. A fee, known as a 'garnish', had to be paid on entering the prison and all essentials – food, soap, candles etc had to be purchased from the guards. Prisoners could also pay to have the heavy and constricting manacles, which were secured to the floor, that all prisoners wore, exchanged for lighter ones or even removed altogether, a privilege known as

BELOW: A view of prisoners exercising in the yard at Newgate, 1872. Taken from *London: A Pilgrimage*, by Blanchard Jerrold and Gustave Doré.

'easement of irons'. Money also changed hands for the right to walk around.

Money also determined where prisoners would be housed. Those without any means of payment could only sleep on the floor without cover and in tiny spaces. In 1753, 300 people were locked up in two rooms a mere 3.4m (11ft) wide and 4.3m (14 ft) long. There were so many lice that, as prisoners walked across their cells, their shells could be heard crackling underfoot. Disease, especially typhus, was rife and killed far more people than the gallows ever did.

If a prisoner had money, on the other hand, he would have a private cell, with a cleaning woman and even a visiting prostitute.

Getting out of Newgate was not easy, even when a sentence was completed, a fee had to be paid before a prisoner would be allowed out. Even if he had died, his family had to pay to have the corpse released. The stench of rotting corpses, whose families did not have the wherewithal to remove them, added to the overall smell of decay that polluted the air around Newgate.

Women prisoners often swapped sex for food, becoming pregnant and having children, who lived inside Newgate. Becoming pregnant was not all bad, as it enabled women to 'plead the belly', which could prevent them being hanged.

Public executions had traditionally taken place at Tyburn, but moved to Newgate in 1783, taking place in the street outside the prison building. Executions drew large crowds, but, for those who wanted an inside view of the prison, a permit could be obtained from the Lord Mayor of London for a visit.

A total of 1,169 people were put to death at Newgate or close to it, between 1783 and 1902, the year it was demolished to make way for the central criminal court, known as the Old Bailey. Of these, 49 were women.

Jail sentences were not seen as an effective crime deterrent, and execution or transportation were the preferred means. After 1660, and the restoration of the

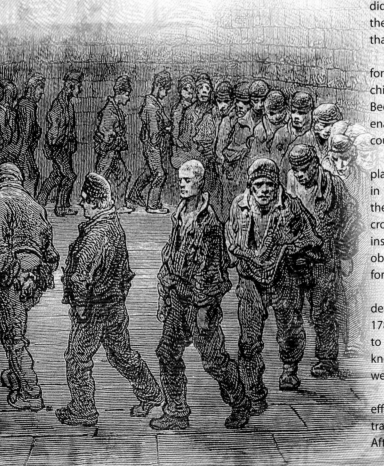

monarchy, the number of crimes for which you could be executed in England rocketed until, by 1815, there were no fewer than 288. These included stealing anything worth more than five shillings (25 pence or 50 cents), going armed in disguise, forging bank notes, cutting down trees, stealing sheep and poaching fish. This litany of crimes, punishable by death, later known as the 'Bloody Code', started to decrease in the 1820s.

All hangings took place on a portable gallows drawn up outside the prison's Debtor's Door. The Cato Street conspirators, who had plotted to kill the Cabinet, were hanged and beheaded there, although their actual sentence was the customary one given for treason – hanging, drawing and quartering.

There were a number of executioners. From 1771 to 1786, Edward Dennis carried out 201 hangings as well as the last instance of burning at the stake when, in 1786, Phoebe Harris, Margaret Sullivan and Catherine Murphy were burned for 'coining', (forging currency). They were lucky enough to have been hanged first, however. On one memorable day, 2 February 1785, Dennis hanged no fewer than 20 men. His assistant, William Brunskill, succeeded him and was responsible for dispatching a remarkable 537 people at Newgate.

The gallows had two parallel beams, allowing a maximum of a dozen people to be hanged at once. The platform on which they stood measured 3m x 2.5m (10ft x 8ft) and was released by moving a lever that released a bar under the drop of between 0.3m-0.6m (1-2 ft). Consequently, people were often slowly strangled to death, rather than dying of a broken neck.

Other notable hangmen included Thomas Cheshire, known, for obvious reasons, as 'Old Cheese'. He officiated at a quadruple hanging in 1829. Another hangman, William Calcraft, had sold pies at hangings and, having become friendly with his two predecessors, was offered the job.

The last man to be publicly executed outside Newgate and, indeed, in Britain, was Michael Barrett, on 26 May 1868. After that, executions took place within the walls of the prison and outside a black flag was raised to signal that the hanging had been carried out.

BELOW: The platform and gallows at Newgate Prison, in 1783.

LEMP MANSION
3322 DEMENIL PLACE,
ST LOUIS, MISSOURI, USA

THE LEMP MANSION AT 3322 DEMENIL
PLACE, ST LOUIS, WAS ONCE A BEAUTIFUL
PROPERTY, BOUGHT BY WILLIAM J
LEMP IN 1876 WITH PROCEEDS FROM
HIS EXTREMELY SUCCESSFUL BREWERY
BUSINESS. WHEN THEY MOVED IN,
THE FAMILY WERE RIDING HIGH, BUT
IN THE YEARS THAT FOLLOWED, THE
LEMPS' LUCK TOOK A SEVERE TURN
FOR THE WORSE.

These days, the Lemp mansion is a restaurant and an inn, behind which stands what remains of the famous Lemp brewery. It once covered ten city blocks, but is now derelict. The mansion was once a fabulous place. In its underground caves it boasted an auditorium, a ballroom and a swimming pool built in a natural cavern. A tunnel led from the brewery to the house, inside which visitors would have been delighted by beautiful, expensive furniture, hand-painted ceilings, Italian marble, carved wood detailing and an art collection to die for.

Much of the house is now empty or sealed up, but there are many who believe the Lemps never left, even when they died, usually by their own hand. Reports of gunshot sounds, screams, laughing, crying and voices calling out names have served to make the Lemp mansion one of America's most haunted houses. And it is no wonder, because the Lemps were a family cursed with a uniquely tragic history.

The 33-roomed Lemp mansion was built in 1868 by a St. Louis inhabitant, Jacob Fleickert and, in 1876, William J Lemp and his wife, Julia moved in. 78 years previously, Johann 'Adam' Lemp was born, in Gruningen, in Germany. Moving to the US, he had become a naturalized citizen in 1841. He was a grocer who also made beer but, by 1840, he had given up the grocery side of his affairs and focused on brewing and selling beer at his Western Brewery in St. Louis. There were around 40 breweries in the city at the time and Lemp's was one of the most successful. So successful, in fact, that, by the time of his death, he was a millionaire.

Adam's son, William J Lemp, took over the brewery on his father's death, initiating the construction, in 1864, of a larger brewery that would become one of the biggest in the country. He installed the first refrigeration machine in an American brewery and introduced the idea of refrigerated railway carriages so that his beer could be the first to be sold nationally. Soon, it was being exported and sold all over the world.

In 1892, the Western Brewery changed its name to the William J Lemp Brewing Company, of which William became president and his son, William Jr, vice-president. William Jr, known as Billy, had gone to St. Louis University, like his father, but William Sr wanted to pass the business on to his fourth son, Frederick. However, when Frederick died in 1901, aged only 28, it was a devastating blow to William Sr, who slowly began to fall apart. At 9.30 am on 13 February 1904, he shot himself in the head in one of the mansion's upstairs bedrooms. He died 45 minutes later, leaving Billy to take over.

Billy had married the beautiful Lillian Hanlan, a wealthy woman in her own right, four years earlier. Lillian became known as the 'Lavender Lady', because of her fondness for dressing in clothes of that colour. Even her carriage horses' harnesses were dyed lavender. Unfortunately, Billy was something of a playboy and threw lavish parties in the storage caves

BELOW: William Lemp Jr.

beneath the mansion, to which he invited prostitutes to entertain his numerous, wastrel friends. It has been reported that Billy had an illegitimate son by one of these prostitutes. This child was said to suffer from Down's syndrome and was kept locked out of sight in the attic of the great house.

Eventually, Lillian grew weary of Billy's philandering. She divorced him, retaining custody of their son, William Lemp III. For once, on the final day of the divorce proceedings, Lillian did not wear lavender. She appeared in front of the judge clad in black, from head to foot.

The brewery began to go into decline. Competition was fierce and Billy neglected his duties, allowing equipment to deteriorate and failing to keep up with new developments in brewing technology. He married for a second time and, by 1915, had retreated to a mansion he had built on the Merrimac River.

When Prohibition arrived in 1919, the brewery closed, the workers only learning about the closure when they turned up for work one day to find the gates locked. The buildings were sold for $588,000 (£294,000). Prior to Prohibition, they had been estimated to be worth $7 million (£3.5 million).

Then, on 20 March 1920, distressed by her failing marriage, Billy's sister, Elsa Lemp Wright, shot herself, just as her father had done. Billy is reported to have commented on arriving at the house where she had killed herself: 'That's the Lemp family for you.' He slipped further into depression as a result and, on 22 December 1922, he became the third member of his family to shoot himself. His weapon of choice was a .38-calibre revolver and he carried out the act in his office in the mansion where his father had killed himself 18 years earlier.

Tragically, in 1943, his son, William Lemp III, died of a heart attack at the age of 42.

All that remained were Billy's two brothers, Charles and Edwin, who had never worked in the family business. Charles had made his money from banking and real estate and, having refurbished the mansion, he moved back into the old house. But, he became stranger as he got older. He had an obsessive and irrational fear of germs, wore gloves at all times and compulsively washed his hands. He would become the fourth Lemp to commit suicide.

On 10 May 1949, Charles shot his much-loved Dobermann pincher before turning his .38-calibre Colt revolver on himself, on the stairs leading up to his room on the mansion's second floor. He left a note saying, 'St Louis Mo/May 9, 1949, In case I am found dead blame it on no one but me. Ch A Lemp'. It was the only suicide note left by any members of the Lemp family.

After working in the brewery until 1913, Edwin, the last in the Lemp line, had led a quiet life at his estate in Kirkwood, Missouri, where he had an observation tower, two servants' houses, a collection of birds, antelope, sheep, yaks and many other animals. He devoted himself to charitable causes, most notably the St. Louis Zoo.

Before he died, in 1970, Edwin instructed his caretaker to destroy his art collection and all Lemp family heirlooms, perhaps in order to destroy the curse that had so tragically decimated his family.

170   170

160

150

BANGKWANG
CENTRAL PRISON
NONTHABURI PROVINCE, THAILAND

OF ALL THE PRISONS IN ALL THE WORLD, BANGKWANG IS THE MOST NOTORIOUS. DANGEROUSLY OVER-CROWDED, CRAWLING WITH PARASITES AND DISEASE, AND CHOCK-FULL OF DRUG SMUGGLERS AND VIOLENT CRIMINALS - THIS PRISON HAS MORE IN COMMON WITH NEWGATE GAOL OF 18TH CENTURY LONDON, THAN ANY MODERN-DAY WESTERN PRISON. THE BANGKOK HILTON IS ONE PLACE IN THAILAND NO ONE WANTS TO VISIT.

The Thais call it the 'Big Tiger', because, they say, it eats you up. Westerners call it 'the Bangkok Hilton', although that name is used to describe several Thai prisons. This one holds around 7,000 murderers, rapists and drug smugglers, all of whom are in for a minimum of 25 years. It is, quite simply, the most notorious prison in the world – the Bangkwang Central Prison.

Its history goes back as far as 1902, when Thailand's King Rama V bought an extensive piece of land in Bangkok on which he planned to construct a prison for the very worst of Thailand's convicts – prisoners whose appeals were pending in the appeal court and supreme court, convicted male prisoners facing sentences of at least 25 years and prisoners who had been sentenced to death and were awaiting execution. However, it was not until after Rama V's death that building began, in 1927, during the reign of his successor, Rama VI. It was completed in 1931. Today it covers around 32 hectares (80 acres) with 11 dormitories and 11 dining halls. Its perimeter walls are 2,406m (7,894 ft) long, 6m (19.5ft) high, go down 1m (3ft) underground and are equipped with high-voltage wires to deter escape attempts. The walls separating each of the prison's 13 sections are 1.3m (4.3ft) long, 6m (20ft) high and bristle with barbed wire.

When prisoners first arrive at Bangkwang they are put into leg-irons, and these must be worn for the first three months of every sentence. Condemned prisoners, however, wear the leg-irons permanently, they are actually welded on. The authorities do not provide food, and as prisoners have to purchase their own supplies from the prison canteen, money or supplies brought in by visitors are vital to survival. Each prisoner has an account with the canteen and this is managed with a chit system. If a prisoner has no money, he will perform tasks for a prisoner who has money and will earn enough for food and cigarettes that way. Even though many of the inmates are there for drug offences, drugs are still dealt in prison to make money, often smuggled in inside food parcels. Cooking facilities are provided and the authorities provide the gas with which to cook.

Living quarters are barbaric, to say the least. Bangkwang is severely overcrowded following a government clampdown on the drug trade, and there are 24 men to a room, all crammed in and having to sleep on the floor. One inmate reports that if you get up in the night to visit the toilet, you are liable to lose your sleeping space and have to spend the night awake. The guards are unlikely to help, as they are hugely outnumbered by the prisoners. The ratio is, in fact, one guard to every 50 prisoners. To even things out a little, well-behaved prisoners are selected to become 'Blueshirts'. These men are given uniforms and clubs, and can discipline prisoners who step out of line. If even that does not prove to be a deterrent, there is always 'The Jungle', the prisoners' name for solitary confinement. Prisoners can spend months here, with even less facilities than in the rest of the prison – a hole in the ground for waste and no sink.

BELOW: A prison guard demonstrates the chosen method of execution at Bangkwang prison, during a first-ever visit by foreign journalists to the maximum security facility in 9 February 1996.

ABOVE: Prison officers blindfold two condemned inmates, while they await execution by machine gun at Bang Kwang Central Prison.

Roll-calls are carried out twice a day to ensure that no one has escaped, but there is little opportunity for that, given that lock-down occurs at 3.30pm and prisoners spend 15 hours a day locked up.

The prison hospital does not even provide any relief. The Bangkok Hilton is riddled with serious disease – HIV, full-blown AIDS and tuberculosis – but there is little help for the victims who lie shackled to their beds. Hospitals in Thailand rely on charity and the Thai people, believing that Bangkwang prisoners deserve everything they get, refuse to make the necessary donations. Consequently, medicines and treatment are totally inadequate.

The worst thing to be in Bangkwang, of course, is a condemned man. A couple of years ago, there were more than 800. It is bad enough to be waiting to die, but at Bangkwang you never know when, as the authorities do not tell prisoners when their sentences are going to be carried out. The most warning they get is two hours. At least nowadays it is carried out by lethal injection. Until the 1930s, condemned prisoners were beheaded. If the prisoner happened to be of royal lineage, however, the bad news was that he was beaten to death with a lump of wood. The good

news was that the wood had to be sweet-smelling.

In 1932, they switched to machine-gunning the prisoner to death. The condemned man, or woman would be tied to a post, facing away from the machine-gunner, so that he, or she, would not know the identity of his killer and return to haunt him when dead. He would then be shot in the heart from behind. The execution chamber, to this day, bears splatters of dried blood on its walls from those decades of bloody execution. The year 2003, saw a change to lethal injection but only because the machine-gunning was proving too unreliable and the prisoner often had to be finished off with another bullet.

There are only a few ways to leave Bangkwang Central Prison. You leave when you have served your term of imprisonment, having survived the privations on offer. Or, if you behave, you might be released on parole after serving two-thirds of your sentence. Occasionally the king celebrates an event or anniversary by providing royal pardons to a number of prisoners. Or, you may leave in a wooden box through the gate known as the Ghost Gate, the day after you have been executed.

COLLINGWOOD MANOR MASSACRE

1740 COLLINGWOOD MANOR HOUSE, DETROIT, USA

TENSIONS WERE ALREADY RUNNING HIGH FOR THOSE INVOLVED IN ORGANIZED CRIME IN DETROIT IN 1931, AND HYMIE PAUL, JOE LEBOWITZ AND JOE SUTKER - OR THE 'TERRORS OF THE THIRD STREET DISTRICT' - AS THEY BECAME KNOWN, WERE NOT MAKING LIFE ANY EASIER. THESE OUT-OF-TOWNERS SIMPLY REFUSED TO PLAY BY THE RULES OF DETROIT'S GANGLAND SCENE. THEY DOUBLE-CROSSED BUSINESS PARTNERS, HIJACKED AND STOLE FROM ALLIES AND ENEMIES, AND ON 16 SEPTEMBER 1931, THEY PAID THE ULTIMATE PRICE.

In prohibition-era America, in 1931, three out-of-towners, Hymie Paul, Joe 'Nigger Joe' Lebowitz, both 31, and 28-year-old Joe 'Izzy' Sutker, arrived in Detroit. They had been employed as hired guns by Harry Shorr and Charles Leiter, bosses of the Oakland Sugar House Gang that enjoyed an affiliation to the infamous Purple Gang that controlled much of Detroit. The trio's job was to provide protection for booze shipments.

Unfortunately, Hymie, Joe and Izzy were not content to just take orders. They opened a bookie's to make some money on the side – a great deal of money. But that was not enough. Before long, in spite of the fact that they also had their own bootlegging operation, they began to hijack other hoods' assignments of illicit hootch, double-crossed customers and reneged on deals. The other players in the Detroit underworld soon grew sick of them.

In an attempt to benefit from local expertise, Hymie, Joe and Izzy hired an experienced gangster, Solomon 'Solly' Levine, to work with them. Levine was well connected with the Purple Gang, having grown up with the Bernstein brothers, Abe and Ray, two of the gang's leading lights.

Things began to unravel when their bookmaking business took a large hit of several hundred thousand dollars to Detroit's East Side Mafia. They were unable to pay out, but decided they could raise money quickly by purchasing whisky, watering it down and selling it on at a profit. No sooner had they done that than the East Side Gang came back, looking for another big pay-out. They bought another 50 gallons of hootch on credit, diluted it and sold it again.

By now, they were in deep trouble, the kind of trouble that could only end one way. Still, they were optimistic that the Legionnaires Convention would reverse their fortunes and they would be able to pay their now considerable debts. So, they spoke to Ray Bernstein, one of the leaders of the Purple Gang, about the money they owed for the whisky they had bought,

BELOW: The murder scene, as depicted by the *Detroit Times*.

ABOVE: A *Detroit News* photographer hid in a coal elevator to get this picture of rumrunners loading their cars at the foot of Riopelle in 1929.

asking him to give them until at least after the convention. Bernstein came back to them, suggesting a meeting at which they could thrash out a plan. He hinted that they could work for the Purple Gang again once everything was sorted out. The trio relaxed a little.

The meeting was fixed for 3pm on 16 September at 1740 Collingwood Manor House, apartment 211. The night before, Izzy and Hymie took some time off from the bookmaking business, Izzy entertaining his eighteen-year-old girlfriend, drinking the night away with her and listening to music. Hymie went on a bender, but, in the morning he regretted the hangover with

which he woke up and went to work.

The three men left for their appointment at 2.45pm decided to leave their guns behind. This was, after all, a peace conference.

The apartment was situated in a quiet, residential area on Detroit's West Side. The houses stood silently as they parked their car outside the building close to 3pm. They rang the doorbell and, after a few moments, the door was opened by a smiling and welcoming Ray Bernstein. They shook hands, exchanged greetings and he ushered them in. They could hear a gramophone playing, but it was switched off abruptly as they entered the apartment.

They exchanged more pleasantries with Irving Milberg, Harry Keywell and Harry Fleischer – the three Purple Gang luminaries they met inside. These were serious players, the three out-of-towners realised. Keywell was rumoured to have been the lookout on the day of the infamous St Valentine's Day Massacre and Fleischer was a fugitive from the law, a 29-year-old killer whose rap-sheet included assault with intent to kill, armed robbery, kidnapping and receiving stolen property. Milberg was a proven crack-shot who had committed every crime in the book.

Hymie, Joe and Solly made themselves comfortable on a sofa in the living room while Izzy perched on the arm. They made small talk until Fleischer asked Bernstein, 'Where is that guy with the books?' They were waiting, they said, for an accountant who would do the sums for them. Bernstein said he would go out and look for him. Out in the street, he climbed into a car, switched on the engine and gunned the motor, at the same time sounding the horn. Curtains began to twitch at neighbouring windows.

It was, of course, a signal, and no sooner had the noise begun than Fleischer sprung into action, pulling a gun and firing it straight at Joe Lebowitz. Milberg and Keywell also pulled out weapons, opening fire on Izzy and Hymie, who made desperate efforts to escape. But, they had been taken completely off-guard. Hymie slumped against the side of the sofa, eight bullets lodged in his back and head. He still had a cigar dangling from his fingers. Joe Lebowitz tried to escape along the corridor leading to the bedroom, but fell to the floor, riddled with bullets, a cigar stub still clenched firmly between his teeth. Izzy made it as far as the bedroom, but Irving Milberg demonstrated how good his shooting was with a couple of bullet holes, close together on his forehead.

Solly Levine wondered why he had not been shot as well, but they had merely decided that he would die elsewhere, after spreading the word that he had killed the three men and then had been hit himself.

They pushed him down the back stairs of the Collingwood mansion and into a black 1930 Chrysler. They sped out of the alley at the back of the house and, a few blocks further on, split up. Bernstein, handing the shaken Levine $400.00 (£200.00) and telling him to get back to the bookies. He would see him later, he said.

Levine, as a known associate of the three dead men, was picked up within the hour by the police, and a massive manhunt was launched. Milberg, Keywell and Bernstein were arrested, but Harry Fleischer was never convicted for the murders. He went on the run until 1932.

After a sensational trial the jury took a mere 90 minutes to arrive at its verdict – guilty for all three men and a week later they received life sentences without parole

Irving Milberg died in prison seven years later. Harry Keywell was a model prisoner for 34 years, at which point his life sentence was commuted. He was released in 1965, married, got a job and disappeared. In 1963, Ray Bernstein had a stroke in prison that left him paralyzed on his left side and with impaired speech. He had, like Keywell, been a model prisoner and had taught other inmates after he had gained his own high- school diploma. The parole board took pity on him and released him in 1964. He died two years later.

As for Solly Levine, he became a hunted man. The remaining Purple Gang members wanted revenge. So, the police put him on a boat to France. Unfortunately, however, the French did not want him and sent him back. He then tried to go to Ireland, but while he was trying to get it organised, he disappeared.

OPPOSITE PAGE TOP: A crowd gathers outside the Collingwood Manor apartments.

OPPOSITE PAGE BELOW: Irving Milberg.

BELOW: Police mug shots of Purple Gang members: Sammy Millman and Harry Keywell.

JOHN
BODKIN ADAMS
TRINITY TREES SURGERY
EASTBOURNE, ENGLAND

THE TOWN OF EASTBOURNE, ON
THE SOUTH COAST OF ENGLAND, IS
POPULARLY KNOWN AS A RETIREMENT
TOWN, AND COLOQUIALLY AS 'THE
LAND OF THE SETTING SUN'. IT IS A
PLACE DOMINATED BY ELDERLY PEOPLE,
MANY OF WHOM HAVE UPPED-STICKS
AND COME TO EAST SUSSEX TO SPEND
THEIR LAST DAYS IN PEACE AND
TRANQUILITY. FOR MANY OF DR JOHN
BODKIN ADAMS'S PATIENTS, THOSE
LAST DAYS CAME MUCH SOONER THAN
THEY'D EXPECTED.

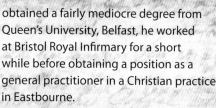

Dr John Bodkin Adams arrived in the English south coast resort of Eastbourne in 1922, where he lived for a few years with his mother and a cousin, Florence Henry. In 1929, however, he took a huge step up in the world when he borrowed £2,000, from one of his patients, William Mawhood, to buy an 18-room house called Kent Lodge. This sizable house was located in an upmarket area of the town, in a street then known as Seaside Road, but which later changed its name to Trinity Trees. It became the venue of many deadly episodes, but for Dr Bodkin Adams, venue was unimportant. He would walk through the doors of many houses in Eastbourne and turn them into houses of death.

Adams's upbringing had been strictly religious. His mother and father had been members of the austere Protestant sect, the Plymouth Brethren, and he remained a member throughout his life. Having

OPPOSITE PAGE: Dr John Bodkin Adams' surgery at Kent Lodge, Trinity Trees, Eastbourne.

BELOW: Mrs Edith Alice Morrell, who died under suspicious circumstances whilst in the care of Doctor John Bodkin Adams.

obtained a fairly mediocre degree from Queen's University, Belfast, he worked at Bristol Royal Infirmary for a short while before obtaining a position as a general practitioner in a Christian practice in Eastbourne.

He gained a terrible reputation and was distrusted by his fellow doctors, who refused to include him in the 'pool system' they devised during World War II to cover for colleagues who had been called up. He had become qualified as an anesthetist in 1941, but, working in the local hospital one day a week, he would fall asleep during procedures and was regarded as dangerously incompetent.

By the mid-30s tongues had already begun to wag about Adams's methods and his relationships with his elderly patients. In 1935, Mrs Matilda Whitton left him £7,385 ($14,770) in her will and he would be included in no fewer than 132 of his patients' wills during the coming years. Eventually, in July 1956, an anonymous telephone call was made to Eastbourne police about him. It was from the well-known music hall performer Leslie Henson, who had become suspicious when his friend, Gertrude 'Bobbie' Hullett, died just four months after her husband. They shared the same doctor, John Bodkin Adams, and Henson had heard the rumours.

People were understandably suspicious. Of the 310 death certificates signed by Bodkin Adams between 1946 and 1956, 163 were found to be suspicious when the police began to examine them. According to a number of the nurses caring for many of the patients he attended, he would ask them to leave the room and gave 'special injections' to the patients, the nature of which he refused to explain.

Fifty year-old 'Bobbie' Hullett, Leslie Henson's friend, had been suicidally depressed since the death of her husband four months previously, and Adams had prescribed her barbiturates. On 19 July 1956, she took an overdose and, as Adams was unavailable, another doctor, Dr Harris, was summoned. When Adams arrived, later that day, and the two doctors conferred,

Adams failed to mention her depression or the medication she had been on. They concluded that she had suffered a cerebral haemorrhage. When a pathologist was asked to take a spinal fluid sample the next day, he suggested that her stomach contents should be looked at to establish whether narcotics were present, but both Adams and Harris rejected the idea. A urine sample, however, showed the presence of 115g (4oz) of sodium barbitone in her body, more than twice the fatal dose. Adams admitted barbiturate poisoning might be a possibility on 22 July and gave Mrs Hullett an antidote – 10cc of Megimide. The recommended dose of Megimide was 100-200cc. As the coroner later said, Adams's treatment was 'merely a gesture'. He also neglected to give her oxygen, although the nurse present described the patient as 'blue', and he failed to put her on an intravenous drip, even though the nurse claimed she was 'sweating a good deal' and losing fluids. Following her death,

A urine sample showed the presence of 115g (4oz) of sodium barbitone in her body, more than twice the fatal dose the inquest found that Mrs Hullett had committed suicide and Adams was cleared of criminal negligence.

Needless to say, Adams benefitted greatly from 'Bobbie' Hullett's will, receiving another Rolls-Royce, worth around £3,000 ($6,000). She had also given him a cheque to the value of £1,000 ($2,000) six days before she died. He asked for it to be specially cleared by the bank, in spite of the fact that Mrs Hullett was one of the richest women in Eastbourne. He wanted his money.

More horror stories emerged. Edith Alice Morrell, for instance, was a wealthy widow who had suffered a stroke. He gave her huge doses of heroin and morphine to help her sleep. In her will he received a small lump sum, a Rolls-Royce Silver Ghost and silver cutlery worth £276 ($552). He had her cremated, having stated on the form that he had no financial interest in her estate. He

had seen her 321 times during her illness, but billed her estate for 1,100 visits.

Emily Louise Mortimer died, aged 75, in 1946, and Adams benefited to the tune of £1,950 ($3,900).

In 1950, 76-year-old Amy Ware left him £1,000 ($2,000), even though he wrote on the cremation form that he was not a beneficiary of her will.

Later that same year, 89-year-old Annabelle Kilgour went into a coma shortly after Adams had started her on a course of sedatives. She left him £200 ($400) and a clock.

In 1952, 85-year-old Julia Bradnum died, leaving him £661($1,322). He had accompanied her to the bank to check her will and gave her advice about changing it. The day before she passed away, she had been fit and well. The next morning, when she said she felt unwell, he gave her an injection, saying, 'It will be over in three minutes.' How right he was.

Shortly before 72-year-old Julia Thomas died, in November 1952, Adams told her cook, 'Mrs Thomas promised me her typewriter. I'll take it now.'

87-year-old Clara Miller left him £1,257 ($2,514) in her will. He would lock her door, throw open the windows, remove her bedclothes and raise her nightgown, exposing her chest to the elements.

There were many more.

Detective superintendent Herbert Hannam of Scotland Yard, famous for solving the infamous 1953 Teddington Towpath Murders, led the police investigation. He faced problems from the start. The British Medical Association (BMA) informed all its members that they should not breach patient confidentiality, even to the police. The Attorney-General, Sir Reginald Manningham-Buller, tried to have the ban rescinded and, amazingly, gave the police's 187-page report to the BMA secretary, Dr Macrae, in order to convince him of the importance of the case. It is likely the report was copied and passed to Adams' defence team.

The case became even more complex when the police came into possession of a

BELOW: Doctor John Bodkin Adams leaves the offices of the General Medical Council, London, 25th November 1959, after they turned down his application to rejoin the Medical Register.

memo by a Daily Mail journalist discussing rumours of homosexuality, illegal at the time, between a police officer, a magistrate and a doctor. The doctor in question was Adams and the magistrate was Sir Roland Gwynne, who was a patient of Adams and visited him every morning at 9am. They were also known to holiday together. The policeman was Richard Walker, chief constable of Eastbourne. The presence of the chief constable's name persuaded Hannam that he should not spend a great deal of time pursuing this line of enquiry.

They arrested Adams, by now, the richest doctor in England, on 19 December 1956. He was charged with the murder of Edith Alice Morrell.

Remarkably, however, after a trial lasting 17 days, Dr John Bodkin Adams was found not guilty.

There were many outside forces involved in the Adams case. It was important, for instance, for the fledgling NHS, which had been founded in 1948. By 1957, disaffection was rife and finances were stretched to breaking point. To have convicted a doctor of murder, and possibly sentenced him to death, would have completely destroyed morale and public confidence in the service. It would also have threatened the future of the government, which was deeply embroiled in the Suez crisis at the time of Adams' arrest.

Interestingly, Adams had treated the 10th Duke of Devonshire, new prime minister, Harold Macmillan's brother-in-law, in 1950, after he suffered a heart attack. The coroner should have been notified when the duke died, as he had not seen a doctor in the 14 days before his death. But Adams signed the death certificate, using a loophole in the law, stating that the duke had died naturally, and therefore avoided the inconvenience of an inquest and the resulting publicity. Macmillan did not want this case to be investigated any further and was grateful to Adams.

Following his acquittal, Adams resigned from the NHS, and later in the year was struck off the medical register when he was convicted of forging prescriptions,

making false statements on cremation forms and three offences under the Dangerous Drugs Act.

He was registered as a doctor again in 1961, suggesting that his colleagues were never entirely convinced of his guilt or his incompetence. In 1983, he fell and fractured his hip while shooting – he was president of the British Clay Pigeon Shooting Association. In hospital, he developed a chest infection and died, leaving an estate valued at £402,970 ($805,490). Those legacies had just kept on coming.

ABOVE: Detective Inspector Brynley Pugh, Head of Eastbourne's Criminal Investigation Department, seen at Eastbourne where he was due to give evidence in the hearing of the case against Dr John Bodkin Adams, 23rd January 1957.

WASHINGTON STATE PENITENTIARY, OR, THE 'CONCRETE MAMA' IS A COLD MISTRESS, KNOWN TO HER INMATES SIMPLY AS 'THE WALLS'. HER FAMOUS RESIDENTS INCLUDE GARY RIDGEWAY - THE GREEN RIVER KILLER, AND KENNETH BIANCHI OF THE HILLSIDE STRANGLERS. SHE IS ALSO HOME TO WASHINGTON STATE'S EXECUTION SUITE, WHERE THE CONDEMNED PRISONER IS PROVIDED WITH A CHOICE BETWEEN DEATH BY LETHAL INJECTION, OR OLD-FASHIONED HANGING.

Sometimes they call it the 'Concrete Mama', a name borrowed from a book of that title. More commonly, it is known as 'Wally World', from the theme park in the Chevy Chase film, National Lampoon's Vacation.

Surrounded by wheat fields, Washington State Penitentiary is located on the outskirts of the town of Walla Walla, famous for its sweet onions and the wine produced by local wineries. It is the state's largest prison, with around 1,800 inmates, and is the site of Washington State's death row, where prisoners await execution. They have a choice. They can make themselves comfortable in the electric chair, or, if they would rather, die by hanging.

Wally World welcomed its first inmates on 11 May 1887. The first ten convicts to take up residence at the new penitentiary were transported from the prison at Seatco in Thurston County, escorted by a company of national guardsmen. The new prison had been built on land donated by the citizens of Walla Walla to replace the old, insecure structure at Seatco. The first prisoner to enter the prison was William Murphy, serving 18 years for manslaughter. Like the rest, he wore a striped suit and his head was shaved.

Discipline has always been rigidly enforced at Walla Walla – in the beginning, prisoners were rarely allowed to speak and when they moved between locations at the prison, they moved in 'lockstep', a method of marching in extremely close, single file, in such a way that the leg of each person in the file moved in the same way and at the same time as the corresponding leg of the person immediately in front. Their legs stayed very close to each other at all times. Nonetheless, two prisoners made the first escape from the new prison just two months after it opened on 4 July, scrambling over the walls. They were recaptured a short distance away and, from then on, guards were positioned on the walls.

Cells at Walla Walla were made of iron, with strap-iron grill doors and, until 1902, the only light was provided by candles. Prisoners had to work and, from 1892, they produced sacks in a one-storey jute mill. From 1921 the factory produced car registration plates. Today, they produce 900,000 plates a year.

Strict silence had to be observed during meal times, and inmates were forbidden from staring at visitors or gazing aimlessly around the dining hall. Guards, too, were under a strict regime. There had to be no 'whistling, scuffing, immoderate laughter or other ungentlemanly conduct' while on penitentiary property.

There have been a number of escape attempts, one of the most unusual of which occurred in 1986, when an inmate had himself sealed inside a tiny cardboard box that measured only 35cm by 48cm by 81cm (14 ins by 19 ins by 32 ins). He left behind a lifelike dummy in his cell to fool the guards. It even wore a wig made from the inmate's own hair. Unfortunately, for him, he was discovered.

In 1891, two inmates were shot dead by a warder after seizing a supply train that

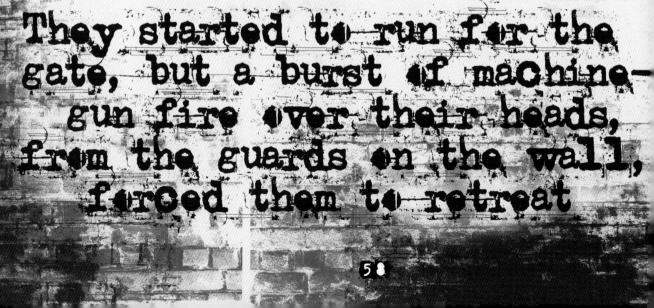

They started to run for the gate, but a burst of machine-gun fire over their heads, from the guards on the wall, forced them to retreat

regularly came into the yard to deliver clay to the prison's brickyard. They captured warder John McLees at knifepoint, but McLees refused to open the gate, instead shouting to a warder on the wall to open fire.

Donald Collins, died in 1933, as he and three other prisoners tried to scale the prison wall after they had broken out through the wall of a vegetable cellar. On the morning of 12 February 1934, the most serious escape attempt took place and it proved to be one of the most disastrous for those involved. Two officers, Floyd Jackson and H M Williams, were seized at knifepoint by inmates Frank Butler and James DeLong, in an office. Other inmates joined them and also seized another warder, Tom Hubbard, who had come in and tried to take the knife away from one of the convicts. Hubbard was stabbed several times and a wire was wrapped around his neck. Jackson was then locked into a cell.

When another warden made a phone call to the office, the inmates forced Jackson to answer and, unknown to the prisoners, he succeeded in communicating to the other man, by the tone of his voice, that all was not well. The warders, now including another three, were forced to lead the prisoners out into the yard. In the meantime, the prison authorities were assembling a team.

As the inmates led the captured warders towards the gate, guards positioned themselves on the walls. En route, however, one warder was fatally stabbed and another was wounded in the leg. Another was almost strangled by wire that had been put around his neck.

This was more than enough for the guards on the wall, who screamed at the prisoners to lie on the ground. When they failed to do so, the men on the wall opened fire. The first shot felled HR Clark, who was serving 10-20 years for killing a man in the prison. Other inmates now rushed out of their workshops to see what the commotion was. They started to run for the gate, but a burst of machine-gun fire over their heads, from the guards on the

wall, forced them to retreat back inside to safety. The prison was placed on lockdown while the warders cleaned up the mess and assessed what had happened.

Seven inmates and one officer lay dead. Four inmates were badly injured and one of them died later from his wounds. It was one of the worst prison death tolls in American history.

BELOW: A prison official walks past the entrance to the upper level of the death chamber at the Washington State Penitentiary in Walla Walla, 1992.

NAZI
DEATH CAMPS
GERMANY, POLAND, AUSTRIA

THE SCALE OF THE GENOCIDE PERPETRATED BY THE NAZIS, AT EXTERMINATION CENTRES SUCH AS AUSCHWITZ AND BELZEC, WAS SO MASSIVE, AND SO HORRIFYINGLY BRUTAL, THAT MANY PEOPLE IN EUROPE COULD NOT BELIEVE HUMAN BEINGS WERE CAPABLE OF SUCH PROFOUND EVIL. THESE HOUSES OF DEATH CONTINUE TO SERVE AS A REMINDER TO US THAT SUCH SICKENING EVENTS MUST NOT BE ALLOWED TO HAPPEN, EVER AGAIN.

The Words *Arbeit Macht Frei* (Work Will Set You Free) are written over the massive iron gates at the entrance to Auschwitz extermination camp. It was one of the last things seen by hundreds of thousands of Jews, gypsies, homosexuals and opponents to Hitler's government. The Nazis placed it there to lull the hordes entering the camp into believing that they were being brought there to work. They were, of course, being brought there to die. The extermination camps set up by Nazi Germany, in the 1940s, represent the ultimate houses of death. They existed purely to exterminate countless numbers of people as quickly and efficiently as possible.

They were part of the plan for what the Nazis termed *Die Endlösung der Judenfrage* – the Final Solution of the Jewish Question – which was concocted and approved at the Nazi Wannsee Conference in January 1942. Control of the extermination programme was given to an enthusiastic young Third Reich *Obersturmbannführer*, Adolf Eichmann. He would organize the largest military operation the world has ever known – the mobilization of tens of thousands of trains to transport the Jews to their deaths.

The Nazis already had camps. These were labour camps – *Arbeitslager* – that were built for the incarceration and forced labour of 'enemies of the state', and later included Jews and prisoners of war. Needless to say, the death rates were still extremely high in these places and inmates died from starvation, disease, exhaustion and extraordinary brutality. Until 1942, the Jews were sent to such concentration camps, places like Dachau and Belsen. From 1942, they went straight to the death camps, and more than half the approximately six million Jews killed in the war died in Hitler's death camps.

They were set-up in a number of locations – Auschwitz, Chelmno, Majdanek, Sobibór, Bełżec, Maly Trostenets and Treblinka. The numbers who died in each of these camps are breathtaking: but may not even tell the whole story. 1,200,000 in Auschwitz; at least 700,000 in Treblinka; around 435,000 in Bełżec; circa 167,000 in Sobibór; between 170,000 and 360,000 at Chelmno; 200,000 at Majdanek and at least 65,000 at Maly Trostenets.

Auschwitz and Chelmno were in parts of western Poland annexed by Germany. Chelmno was ideally located near the city of Lodz, Poland's second-largest city, with a Jewish population of 200,000. At Chelmno, Jews were forced into vans into which tubes were inserted and fed exhaust fumes. It took 15 minutes for the job to be done, and the van would then drop the bodies in pre-dug graves before returning to the camp for the next group. Few people in Poland were even aware that it existed.

Auschwitz-Birkenau is the best known of all the death camps. There were really three camps. At the first one the notorious Josef Mengele carried out medical experiments on twins, dwarves and other unfortunates. But it was Auschwitz II, under the command of the ruthless Rudolf Hoess, that was the extermination camp. The real number of people who died at Auschwitz will never be known, because the Nazis did not register the names of everyone who died there. Built in 1942, it consisted of gas chambers and crematoria for the disposal of the huge numbers of corpses. Around 20,000 were killed every day, resulting in so many corpses that they became a logistical problem.

Trains would arrive daily from all over Europe. On disembarking, the prisoners would be separated into those who looked fit enough to work and those – mostly women and children – who looked unfit. Families were separated from each other during this process.

Those selected for work had their heads shaved and numbers tattooed on their arms, in this way around 400,000 were registered. Around 340,000 of them died as a result of the cruelty they experienced. Those unfit for work went to the gas chambers, at Birkenau, within several hours of their arrival. The cyanide gas Zyklon-B was used, but only after the victims' hair was shaved off for use in making haircloth and gold fillings were removed from teeth to be made into gold bars and sent to Berlin.

As the Russians moved towards Auschwitz, at the end of the war, the Nazis tried to destroy the evidence of what had taken place. When it was liberated, on 27 January 1945, they found a mere 7,600 survivors. Around 58,000 had been sent on a death march to Germany.

Not long after the Germans and Russians had partitioned Poland between them, the Germans built a forced labour camp at Bełżec, housing 11,000. As a forced labour camp, it played host to thousands of deaths from disease, starvation and execution. However, in 1942, it became a death camp, commanded by Odilo Globocnik, the area's police chief, known as Himmler's chief mass murderer. Jews arrived from Poland, Germany, Czechoslovakia and Romania.

Initially diesel fumes were used, but the more efficient Zyklon-B was soon introduced. Late in 1942, however, the killing ceased and the dead, who had been buried in mass graves, were dug up and cremated, in an attempt to destroy the evidence of the horrors that had been perpetrated.

Sobibór was built in 1942, in eastern Poland. It had five gas chambers in which 250,000 Jews from Russia, Poland, Slovakia and western Europe met their deaths. Only 50 prisoners of Sobibór survived the extreme cruelties they faced.

Treblinka was the location of the extermination of the entire Warsaw ghetto. More than 700,000 Jews died there in the same way as at Sobibór and Bełżec. They were told they were being transported to labour camps, but first were ordered to remove their clothing so that they could be bathed and disinfected. They were then gassed – and if they resisted, they were beaten and clubbed with rifle butts. Special work units of Jewish prisoners, known as *Sonderkommandos*, were used to remove gold teeth and dentures from the corpses. They also dealt with the burial and cremation of the victims. When they were too weak to continue working, they, themselves, went to the gas chambers.

The Kommandant of Treblinka, Franz Stangl, was arrested in Brazil, in 1967, and extradited to Germany, where he was sentenced to life imprisonment for the part he played in the murder of 900,000 people. He died six months later.

Majdanek held some non-Jewish prisoners and there was some work done there. However, in October 1942, a crude gas chamber was constructed in a wooden barracks. Later, a more sophisticated chamber was built of concrete, with airtight steel doors. Carbon monoxide gas was used initially, but, as with the other camps, Zyklon-B soon became the preferred method. It is unclear exactly how many died at Majdanek. Some say it may have been as many as 1,380,000. In 1943, as the Russians closed in on Lublin, the camp was being closed. The 17,000 prisoners still held at the camp were shot in an operation euphemistically called Erntefest – Fall Harvest.

BELOW: The charred remains of a prisoner inside Buchenwald cremation oven, placed on display for German civilians, who were forced to view the Nazi atrocities found by American forces after they liberated this camp.

BUGSY SIEGEL
810 LINDEN DRIVE,
Beverly Hills, California

IN THE 1930S AND 40S, 810 LINDEN DRIVE WAS THE PICTURE OF BEVERLY HILLS LUXURY. THE HOUSE WAS RENTED BY BUGSY SIEGEL'S 'MOLL', VIRGINIA HALL, WHO HAPPENED TO BE IN PARIS ON THE NIGHT OF 20 JUNE 1947, WHEN HER LOVER WAS PUMPED FULL OF BULLETS BY A MAFIA HITMAN, INTENT ON SILENCING THE TROUBLESOME MOBSTER ONCE AND FOR ALL.

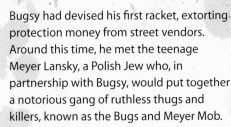

It was 20 June 1947, and Bugsy Siegel was king of the world. He had just returned to the sumptuous villa at 810 Linden Drive in Beverly Hills, having enjoyed a manicure and a haircut, and he was looking forward to a relaxing evening. Finally, things were going well. Business had been ropey for a while and he had not been absolutely certain he would make it, but now the money was rolling in and everything he had promised was coming to pass. What's more, his daughters were on their way to spend the summer with him. What more could a man want?

Meanwhile, outside, in the garden of the house, Charlie Fischetti, a hired killer, squeezed the trigger of his Springfield rifle and the sound of gunfire splintered the hot Las Vegas evening.

At just under 1.8m (6 ft) tall, black-haired and blue-eyed, Bugsy Siegel was the prototype racketeer. He was born Benjamin Siegelbaum, in 1902, to poor immigrant Russian parents and grew up in Brooklyn's tough Williamsburg area. By his early teens

BELOW: American mobster Benjamin 'Bugsy' Siegel lighting a cigar.

Bugsy had devised his first racket, extorting protection money from street vendors. Around this time, he met the teenage Meyer Lansky, a Polish Jew who, in partnership with Bugsy, would put together a notorious gang of ruthless thugs and killers, known as the Bugs and Meyer Mob.

The gang contained men who would later become some of America's most notorious gangsters – Abner 'Longy' Zwillman, Lepke Buchalter, future head of the infamous Murder Inc. – the only Mob leader ever to die in the electric chair – and Arthur Flegenheimer, later to achieve notoriety as Dutch Schultz.

Meyer soon realized that it would be better to have the Sicilian gangs on his side. So, he and upcoming Sicilian gangster, Charlie 'Lucky' Luciano, forged an invaluable link. It was for Luciano, in fact, that Bugs and Meyer carried out their first hit when they killed the son of an Irish cop who had set Luciano up on a narcotics charge.

By 1919, the Bugs and Meyer Mob was making its money from floating crap games, trade unions and robbery. However, the big time was where their ambitions lay. They put aside money from robberies and their craps and protection rackets, money they invested in established bookmaking businesses and also found its way into the pockets of Lower East Side politicians and policemen who could provide them with protection to carry on their business.

When the Volstead Act became law in 1919, making the manufacture and sale of alcohol illegal in the United States, it was a red-letter day for racketeers everywhere, but especially for Luciano, Lansky and Siegel.

From about 1927 – 1931, the warring factions of the New York underworld went head to head and the Castellamarese war, as it came to be called, between Mafia bosses, Joe Masseria and Sal Maranzano, would define organized crime in America for decades to come. When Luciano changed his sympathies and went over to Maranzano's side, he did so on the understanding that he would deal with Joe Masseria.

AMERICA'S MONTE CARLO

the Flamingo HOTEL

75 Minutes by Air
To Gay LAS VEGAS

GRAND OPENING
AMERICA'S FINEST RESORT HOTEL

MARCH 1

With The

ANDREWS SISTERS

and

HENRY KING'S
ORCHESTRA

FOR HOTEL AND DINING ROOM
RESERVATIONS WIRE OR PHONE
LAS VEGAS 4000

LAS VEGAS

On 15 April, 1931, he invited Masseria to Scarpato's Restaurant in Coney Island. Towards the end of the meal, Luciano excused himself and went to the bathroom. As he closed the door, four gunmen burst into the room, guns blazing. They were Albert Anastasia, Vito Genovese, Joe Adonis and, leading the charge, as ever, Bugsy Siegel. Masseria was hit six times and another 14 bullets lodged themselves in the restaurant walls.

Charlie Luciano completed his rise to the top by rubbing out Sal Maranzano. Bugsy, however, was never one to abide by the rules and, after one murder too many for which he had not obtained the permission of his superiors, he was becoming too

much of a liability. But, the National Crime Syndicate liked him and decided to give him another chance. He was sent to the West Coast where the Mob's influence was nowhere near as great as in the east.

Bugsy arrived in California with his wife and kids, and bought a $200,000 (£100,000) mansion in the upmarket area of Holmby Hills. He began moving in elite circles, hanging out with George Raft, an old friend from Williamsburg who had become a major movie star. Raft provided Bugsy with a ticket into the high-octane world of Hollywood's movie stars and starlets. With his suave good looks, he began to occupy the gossip columns, attending parties and premieres.

ABOVE: A coroner's assistant covers the bullet-ridden body of Benjamin 'Bugsy' Siegel, the mafia gangster and underworld big shot who was slain by five of nine bullets fired through a window into his Beverly Hills mansion.

But, Bugsy was also busy during the day. He infiltrated the unions and began to make serious money for the Mob. However, he could not be kept away from the action and, on more than one occasion, became more involved in a situation than a man of his high status should have been. In 1939, when Harry 'Big Greenie' Greenberg was eliminated in California, Bugsy was in it up to his neck. As one of his cohorts said, 'We all begged Bugsy to keep out of the shooting. He was too big a man by this time to become personally involved. But Bugsy wouldn't listen.'

He had got under the Syndicate's skin once too often, but Las Vegas was his last hurrah. In 1931, the Nevada legislature had legalized gambling to raise revenue. In the 1940s, it also legalized off-track betting on horse races. This was what interested Bugsy. Opening a legitimate casino in Vegas had unlimited of potential for making money for the Mob. He resolved to open a casino-hotel in the one-horse town of Las Vegas. He called it the Flamingo.

Right from the beginning, the Flamingo proved to be a money-pit. He was ripped off by construction workers and the money he needed to complete the hotel grew from $1 million (£500,000) to $6 million (£3 million). His Mob investors became twitchy.

By 1946, the hotel had still not opened its doors and Bugsy was asking for even more money. Finally, at a Mafia conference in Havana, Cuba, on 22 December that year, Meyer Lansky delivered some bad news. Bugsy had been skimming from the cash provided by the Mob for the Flamingo. He was thought to be depositing it in Swiss bank accounts, ready to flee if all did not go according to plan. The Syndicate turned to Lansky and asked him what they should do. He reluctantly told them that Bugsy had to be hit, a motion that was passed unanimously, and the contract was given to Charlie Fischetti. Lansky, nonetheless, provided his old friend with a stay of execution, persuading them that the contract should be delayed until after the opening of the casino – Boxing Day – to see what happened. Who knows, he suggested, it might even be a huge success and they could get Siegel to pay back the money.

In spite of top-notch entertainment – George Raft, Jimmy Durante, Xavier Cugat's orchestra, all big names back then – and the presence at the opening of movie stars Clark Gable, Lana Turner, Joan Crawford and many more, the Flamingo was a flop.

It was with a heavy heart that Lansky reported the troubling situation in Las Vegas, and the Syndicate demanded the fulfilment of the contract. Nonetheless, he gained another stay of execution and the Flamingo limped along until Bugsy closed it to enable the hotel part of his complex to be finished.

It reopened in March and by May it had returned a healthy profit of $250,000 (£125,000). But it was all too late for the Syndicate.

Charlie Fischetti's first bullet hit Bugsy Siegel in his handsome head as he lolled on his sofa and another four rammed into him in quick succession, smashing his ribs and destroying his lungs.

Aged 42, Benjamin 'Bugsy Siegel' Siegelbaum, who had been born in the slums of Brooklyn, and had once owned a 35-room mansion in Hollywood, was dead.

His memorial stands, shimmering to this day, in the Nevada desert – the gambling capital of the world – the city of Las Vegas.

IN LOVING MEMORY FROM THE FAMILY

BENJAMIN SIEGEL
FEB. 28, 1906
JUNE 20, 1947

PENTONVILLE PRISON

CALEDONIAN ROAD,
NORTH LONDON, ENGLAND

PENTONVILLE PRISON WAS BUILT IN THE STYLE OF EASTERN STATE PENITENTIARY, AND HAD THE SAME EFFECT ON MANY OF ITS INMATES. SOME WENT MAD, SOME BECAME DELUSIONAL AND SOME COMMITTED SUICIDE. THE DEHUMANIZING TACTICS USED BY THE PRISON AUTHORITIES WERE SIMPLY TOO MUCH FOR SOME PEOPLE TO BEAR.

The bad news for prisoners arriving at the Model Prison, in the 19th century, was that the system for controlling them was borrowed from the harsh regime in operation at America's Eastern State Penitentiary, sometimes known as the 'separate system'. Inmates were forbidden from communicating with each other and when exercising or being taken anywhere in the prison grounds, had to march rapidly, in straight lines, close to each other, wearing masks of brown cloth on their faces. This dehumanizing effect was carried through to their daily attendance at chapel, when each man sat in a tiny cubicle, his head visible to the warder, but not to his fellow inmates. The result, as in Eastern State, was mental illness. One study found that for every 60,000 prisoners at Pentonville 220 went mad, 210 became delusional and 40 committed suicide.

The day was hard. Work began at 6am and continued until 7pm. Prisoners would weave or make rope and they enjoyed only paltry rations. For breakfast there was 284g (10 oz) of bread and 355ml (0.75 pints) of cocoa. Dinner was a 237ml (0.5 pints) of soup or 114g (4oz) of meat, 142g (5oz) of bread and 454g (1lb) of potatoes. Then, for supper they would have 473ml (1 pint) of

BELOW: An engraving depicting a separate cell in Pentonville Prison.

gruel – oatmeal boiled in water –and 142g (5oz) of bread. In the 1840s, it cost around 15 shillings (75 pence or $1.50) a week to feed and house a prisoner in Pentonville. However, it was a system much admired for its effectiveness and its cost. A further 54 prisons were constructed in the UK based on the Pentonville model, and many throughout the British Empire.

Pentonville was a hanging prison, and successful applicants for the job of hangman were trained there. They attended a one-week course that included lessons such as how to calculate and set the drop, using tables of measurement provided by the Home Office, how to pinion the condemned man and, critically, how to expedite the entire process. Everything was practiced using a dummy called 'Old Bill'.

Apprentice hangmen met Old Bill on the second day of the course, the first being taken up with a medical, an interview with the governor and a tour of the execution shed. Using Old Bill, they learned how to put the white hood on and how to get the eyelet of the noose in exactly the right place. This was essential for what was termed the system of 'humane hanging'. They repeated the process over and over until it was second nature – putting on the hood, adjusting the noose, pulling out the safety pin, pushing the lever and watching the prisoner drop. They were also shown how to manage double executions.

Every eventuality was catered for – prisoners with only one leg or arm and a prisoner who had attempted suicide by cutting his throat, for example.

The last two hangmen to be trained in this way were Samuel Plant and John Underhill, who took the course in 1960, remaining on the list of hangmen until they were rendered redundant by the abolition of the death penalty in the UK in 1965. The most prolific hangman in Pentonville's history was Albert Pierrepoint, the third man in his family to be a hangman. Of the total of 433 men and 17 women he hanged between 1932 and 1955, 43 were carried out at Pentonville.

In the 20th century, more hangings were carried out at Pentonville than at any other British prison. There were 120 hangings altogether there between 1902 and 1961 – 112 for murder, two for treason and six for spying during wartime.

The first man to be hanged there was John Macdonald, who stabbed another man to death over five shillings (25 pence or 50 cents). But it had its share of famous executions over the years.

Dr Hawley Harvey Crippen was perhaps one of the most sensational murderers in English criminal history. Crippen murdered his wife, Belle, and fled with his mistress, Ethel Le Neve, to Canada on the SS Montrose. On board, he was recognized by the ship's captain from a newspaper photograph and a telegraph message was sent, informing the ship's owners, who alerted Scotland Yard; the first time a ship to shore telegraph had been used in a criminal case. Crippen was arrested and found guilty of murder, while Le Neve was acquitted. He was hanged at 9am on 23 November 1911, by John Ellis, and his last request was to be allowed to have a picture of his lover, Ethel Le Neve in his jacket pocket. Ellis recorded in his memoirs that Crippen smiled as he walked towards him.

The execution of the poisoner John Sedden, on 18 April 1912, was one of the fastest on record, taking just 25 seconds. En route to the gallows, it seemed as if the condemned man was about to faint at the sight of the noose. A passing tourist bus also sounded its horn at that moment, further frightening him. Again, John Ellis was the executioner.

Ellis hanged Irish revolutionary Sir Roger Casement, for treason, on 3 August 1916. Casement, who was Irish by birth, but crucially held a British passport, had solicited help from Germany for the Easter uprising in Ireland, in 1916. However, the British intercepted a message he sent to his Irish colleagues and, after returning to Ireland on board a German submarine, he was arrested and taken to London and tried for conspiring with Britain's enemies during a time of war. His trial lasted just three days, and shortly before his execution was stripped of his knighthood.

Six spies were hanged at Pentonville during World War II and 27 year-old Private John Schurch was executed, in 1946, for treachery, the last person to be hanged in Britain for an offence other than murder. A member of Oswald Mosley's British Union of Fascists, prior to the war, Schurch was captured by the Germans in Tobruk and began working for both Italian and German intelligence. He would pose as a captured prisoner-of-war to gain the trust of fellow Allied prisoners. He was the only British soldier to be executed for treachery during World War II.

Among other well-known executions were those of Neville Heath, who killed two women, sadistically, in 1946; Timothy Evans and John Reginald Christie, who were hanged in 1950 and 1953 in a sensational case, and the last double-hanging in Britain, when 22-year-old Kenneth Gilbert and 24-year-old Ian Grant were executed for a murder during the course of a robbery they were carrying out.

BELOW: Dr Hawley Harvey Crippen was found guilty of the murder of his wife Belle Ellmore after fleeing with his lover to Canada. He was hanged at Pentonville Prison in 1910.

JOHN REGINALD CHRISTIE

10 RILLINGTON PLACE, NOTTING HILL, LONDON, ENGLAND

10 RILLINGTON PLACE, AS FAR AS THE BRITISH COURTS ARE CONCERNED, WAS ONCE HOME TO MORE THAN ONE KILLER. TWO TENANTS: TIMOTHY EVANS AND JOHN REGINALD CHRISTIE WERE TRIED AND FOUND GUILTY OF MURDER AND BOTH WERE EVENTUALLY EXECUTED FOR THEIR CRIMES. EVANS EVENTUALLY RECEIVED A POSTHUMOUS PARDON FOR THE MURDER OF HIS YOUNG DAUGHTER, BUT DID HE KILL HIS WIFE, OR WAS CHRISTIE THE REAL CULPRIT? THIS RUN-DOWN THREE-STOREY TERRACE HOUSE IN NOTTING HILL HELD THE ANSWERS.

10 Rillington Place was a small Victorian house, built in the 1860s, when the Notting Hill and North Kensington areas were undergoing development. Located where the elevated dual carriageway, the Westway runs today, number 10 was located in a row of three-storey terraced houses. The house was split into three flats, none of which had a bathroom. Instead, an outhouse in the garden was used by the occupants of all three flats, and a wash house was also located there for the use of tenants, but it was not always functioning.

John Reginald Christie moved into the ground floor flat at 10 Rillington Place in December 1938 with his wife, Ethel. They were pleased with the flat because, as it was on the ground floor, they would enjoy use of the garden.

Christie had been raised in Halifax, in Yorkshire, but had been unpopular with school friends. He suffered from chronic impotence throughout his life, and it is presumed that this was probably what caused him to commit the terrible crimes for which he was responsible. He was also a hypochondriac, using feigned illnesses to attract attention to himself as well as to avoid work. He had married Ethel in 1920,

BELOW: A chillingly accurate waxwork of John Reginald Halliday Christie, representing the murderer in the kitchen of 10 Rillington Place, Notting Hill, London.

but the marriage failed and they separated. Ten years later, however, they got back together, moving to London to start afresh.

Christie, while separated from Ethel, had been convicted and imprisoned several times for petty criminal offences – stealing postal orders while employed as a postman, car theft and assaulting a prostitute. Strangely, at the outbreak of World War II, this raft of offences did not prevent him from becoming a policeman. Neither did his reconciliation with his wife prevent him from continuing to sleep with prostitutes, especially when Ethel was away visiting relatives.

In April 1948, Timothy Evans and his pregnant wife, Beryl, moved into the top-floor flat at 10 Rillington Place and six months later, Beryl gave birth to a daughter, Geraldine. Evans was a Welshman of limited intelligence, who worked as a lorry driver. He and his wife often engaged in loud and sometimes violent arguments, mostly over Beryl's inability to make ends meet. Matters were made worse in late 1949, when she informed her husband that she was pregnant again.

Beryl insisted immediately that she wanted an abortion, but Evans, a Roman Catholic, was against the idea. She, however, confided in Christie and, although he had absolutely no previous experience, he told her that he knew how to carry out abortions, having learned how to do it during the war. He persuaded her to let him carry out the procedure, but it ended disastrously. When Evans came home later that day, 8 November 1949, Christie informed him that Beryl had died during the operation. Christie told Evans that he would dispose of the body down a nearby drain and that he would also find someone to look after the baby, Geraldine. He told Evans to leave London.

Evans returned to Wales, but eventually went to a police station a few weeks later to tell the police that he had disposed of his wife's body after she had taken something to make her abort her baby. The police did not find the body down the drain where Evans said he had put it, but when they searched the wash house at 10 Rillington Place, they found the bodies of both Beryl and baby Geraldine. Evans inexplicably confessed to killing his wife no fewer than four times during lengthy police interrogations.

At Evans's trial, six weeks later, Christie denied that he had agreed to perform an abortion on Beryl, and his testimony, plus Evans's poor performance in the witness box, resulted in a guilty verdict. Timothy Evans was sentenced to death and hanged at Pentonville Prison on 9 March 1950.

In late 1952, Ethel Christie suddenly disappeared. Christie told friends that she had moved back to Sheffield and he was going to join her when he had settled their affairs in London. He gave up his job, sold all his furniture and rented out his flat to a couple. After they had stayed there just one night, however, they learned that the flat was not Christie's to rent and were thrown out. The landlord rented the flat to a Jamaican immigrant named Beresford Brown. Tidying up the kitchen one day, Brown peeled off some wallpaper and discovered a door leading to a pantry. Opening the door slightly, he shone a torch into the space beyond. There, he saw the body of a woman, seated and hunched forward, clad only in bra, stockings and suspenders. He immediately called the police and, when they arrived, they discovered two more women's bodies. They were the bodies of three prostitutes that Christie had lured back to the house and killed while he lived there – Kathleen Maloney, Rita Nelson and Hectorina MacLennan. Searching the remainder of the flat, under the floorboards of the living room they found the remains of Ethel Christie. Christie had strangled her on 14 December 1952. She had been in poor health and Christie later claimed that he merely put her out of her misery.

In the garden, two more women's bodies were discovered – Austrian prostitute Ruth Fuerst and a workmate of Christie's, whose catarrh he had promised he could cure with a special type of inhaler. Bringing her to the flat, he made her breathe in a concoction he

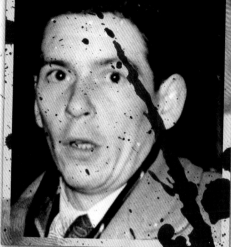

LEFT: Convicted killer Timothy John Evans, hanged for murdering his baby daughter, Gerladine. Evans was granted a posthumous pardon in 1966 when the Brabin report finally concluded that the murder was committed by John Reginald Christie.

had put together in a jar. However, he had connected the jar to the gas supply. As his victim, unknowingly, breathed in the gas and weakened, he strangled her and, as he strangled her, he had intercourse with her.

Christie's impotence, it seemed, only dissipated when he had complete control over the woman with whom he was having sex. Of his first victim, he later said, *'I remember as I gazed down at the still form of my first victim, experiencing a strange, peaceful thrill.'* It was a 'thrill' he would experience six times.

After wandering around London for several weeks, as the entire police searched for him, Christie was finally arrested on Putney Bridge and confessed to the murders. He additionally admitted that he had killed Beryl Evans, but he never confessed to killing her baby, Geraldine. Nonetheless, many thought it highly unlikely that two stranglers could live in the same house.

On 15 July 1953, John Reginald Christie was hanged on the same gallows as Timothy Evans.

Debate about the execution of Evans raged on for years until, in 1966, the Brabin Report concluded that Christie had killed Geraldine Evans and persuaded Timothy Evans not to go to the police. Home secretary, Roy Jenkins awarded Evans a posthumous pardon in the case of Geraldine Evans. However, he has still not been officially declared innocent of the murder of his wife, for which he was never tried.

ED GEIN

GEINS' FARM, PLAINFIELD, WISCONSIN, USA

ED GEIN IS REGARDED BY MANY AS THE MOST NOTORIOUS SERIAL KILLER OF ALL TIME. THE SHOCKING REALITY OF HIS CRIMES MEAN THEY WILL FOREVER BE EMBLAZONED ON THE HISTORY BOOKS. THE BUTCHER OF PLAINFIELD WAS AS DISTURBED AND AS DANGEROUS AS THEY COME. TODAY, THE SITE WHERE THE GEIN FAMILY FARM STOOD IS ALL BUT EMPTY. THE HOUSE ITSELF HAS LONG GONE, BUT SOUVENIR HUNTERS STILL REGULARLY PILLAGE IT FOR BITS AND PIECES OF MEMORABILIA TO SELL ON THE INTERNET.

On 17 November 1957, following a robbery at the hardware store in Plainfield, Wisconsin, in which she worked, Bernice Worden disappeared. Police discovered that the last customer in the store had been Ed Gein, a local man who lived alone in a ramshackle, dilapidated old farmhouse in a desolated location on the outskirts of the small town. They travelled out to the gloomy farm to interview Gein. What they found when they arrived would shock and horrify the nation.

The first thing they noticed was the stench. Decomposing rubbish and rotten junk covered every space, work-surface and littered the floor to the extent that it was difficult to walk. The local sheriff, Arthur Schley, was making his way gingerly through the room with a torch when he felt something brush against him, something hanging from the ceiling beams. He shone his torch upwards into the dark to see a large carcass, hanging upside down, decapitated, the ribcage sliced open and the insides gutted, just like you would a deer, something common to this area where hunting was a popular activity. But this was no deer, the policeman quickly realised to his horror. It was the body of the missing woman, Bernice Worden, who had been shot dead at close range with a .22-calibre rifle. That was not all they found in this charnel house, however.

The bed in Gein's small bedroom had bizarre decorations on each of the four corner posts – human skulls. Gein's home also held more horrors: skin had been used to make a lampshade and to upholster the seats of chairs; sliced off women's breasts were being used as cup holders; human skullcaps were being used as soup bowls; a human heart lay in a saucepan on the cooker; the pull of a window shade was a pair of human lips. There was a mammary vest made of woman's skin; a belt made from human nipples; socks made from human flesh and a box of human vulvas which Gein later admitted to wearing. Finally, they found a suit made entirely of human skin.

At 39 years old, Ed Gein had taken the death of his mother, Augusta, in 1945 pretty badly. His late father had been less than useless and his mother was a strict Lutheran who read Ed and his older brother passages from the Old Testament, to keep them on the straight and narrow. She lectured them that women were wicked and to be avoided at all costs. But there was little chance of Ed being led astray. He had always been a strange boy, laughing randomly at his own private jokes and being bullied for his slightly effeminate manner. He was a loner, as Augusta would not let him make friends but his attachment to her grew into an unhealthy one, a fact commented on by his brother, who was gradually moving away from the kind of life Augusta wanted for him. One day in 1944, during a forest fire, Henry was found dead and, although it was speculated that Ed probably dispatched him, foul play was not suggested at the time.

human skullcaps were being used as soup bowls a human heart lay in a saucepan on the cooker the pull of a window shade was a pair of human lips

When Augusta died, following a series of strokes, Ed was left completely alone. He boarded up his mother's rooms – the upstairs, downstairs parlour and living room – keeping them as a shrine to her memory. He took up residence in the kitchen and a small room off it, which became his bedroom. Here, he spent his time reading about Nazi atrocities, south sea cannibals and, eerily, anatomy. His neighbours, (some of whom he did odd jobs for), spread nasty rumours about him. Some young boys who visited the farm saw shrunken heads, but their parents dismissed the story as childish fantasy. Nonetheless, he was known as 'Weird Ed'.

His favourite hobby was visiting the local cemetery. There, he would dig up the graves of recently buried middle-aged women who looked like his mother. He would drag the bodies home, skin them and tan the skin from which he would make the macabre objects that cluttered his rooms.

Following Augusta's death, Ed decided that he wanted to have a sex change. It was for this reason that he wore the suit made of women's skin, so he could pretend to be his mother rather than have to go through with the operation.

They estimated that Ed had carved up 15 bodies at the farmhouse. Coincidentally, Wisconsin Police had noticed an increase in the 1940s and 1950s in the number of people who had disappeared. An eight-year-old girl, Georgia Weckler, vanished on her way home from school in 1947; in 1952, two hunters stopped for a drink in Plainfield – neither Victor Travis or Ray Burgess were ever seen again. In 1953, Evelyn Hartley was babysitting when she disappeared, leaving her shoes, glasses and bloodstains behind. In the winter of 1954, Plainfield tavern-keeper Mary Hogan disappeared from her bar – again a trail of blood was left behind in the car park. Ed Gein had killed them all.

Gein was found to be mentally incompetent and unfit to be tried for first-degree murder and was committed to the Central State Hospital in Waupun, Wisconsin. Ten years later, however, he was deemed competent to stand trial for the murder of Bernice Worden and was, finally, found guilty of first-degree murder. However, he was judged to have been insane at the time of the crime and was later found not guilty by reason of insanity. They sent him back to hospital where he happily spent the remainder of his life. On 26 July 1984, he lost a long battle with cancer and died. He was buried in Plainfield cemetery next to his mother and close to all the graves he had robbed years before.

After he was convicted, Ed Gein's farm went up in flames. Plainfield's fire department took the call and attended the fire, but it was too late. Perhaps they failed to deal with the incident with a great deal of urgency, given who the fire chief was. His name was Frank Worden and he was the son of Bernice Worden, one of weird Ed's unfortunate victims.

BELOW: The cluttered kitchen of serial killer Ed Gein, where some of his victims' body parts were found.

HOLLOWAY PRISON

LONDON BOROUGH OF ISLINGTON, ENGLAND

HOLLOWAY PRISON, IN LONDON, IS THE LARGEST WOMEN'S PRISON IN EUROPE. IT IS MOST FAMOUS AS THE PLACE WHERE - UNTIL THE ABOLITION OF THE DEATH PENALTY IN 1965 - CONDEMNED WOMEN WERE SENT TO BE EXECUTED. ON 13 JULY 1954, RUTH ELLIS, THE LAST, AND CONSEQUENTLY THE MOST FAMOUS WOMAN TO BE EXECUTED IN THE UK, WAS HUNG IN THE CONDEMNED CELL AT HOLLOWAY.

Holloway Prison was opened in October 1852 as the City of London House of Correction, with 436 cells – 283 for men, 60 for females and 62 for juveniles. There were also 18 punishment cells, 14 reception cells for new arrivals and 14 workrooms where good inmates made use of their incarceration. In 1882, 340 cells were added, and a hospital wing was added a year or so later. It served as London's main prison and also catered for remand prisoners, the most famous of whom was the playwright and poet, Oscar Wilde. Suffragettes who were sent to prison ended up in Holloway.

With the ending of the punishment of transportation and the demolition of Newgate prison to make way for the Old Bailey in 1903, more space was needed for women prisoners in London, and Holloway provided the ideal solution. It was designated an all-woman jail with capacity for 949 women prisoners, rising to over 1,000 two years later.

BELOW: A suffragette on hunger strike is force-fed through the nose during her detention at Holloway Prison. Many members of the medical profession regarded this procedure as highly dangerous.

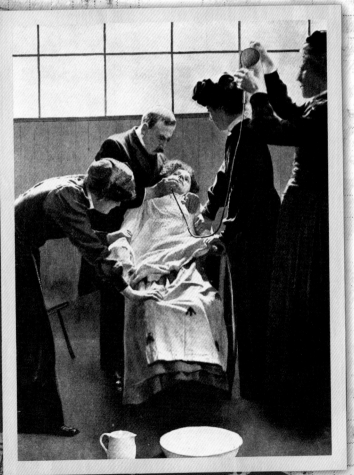

Most notably, Holloway became the venue for the execution of women condemned to death. Among these were the only women ever to be sentenced to death in Britain for spying. Swedish national, Eva de Bournonville, was convicted during the World War I. She was reprieved, however, and served only six years in prison. Dorothy Pamela O'Grady was lucky enough to be reprieved just two days before her death sentence was due to be carried out. She had been accused of cutting a telephone wire on the Isle of Wight and being seen in areas prohibited to the public. She served 14 years in Holloway.

A total of 47 women arrived in Holloway's condemned cell from 1903 until the death penalty was abolished in 1965, although 40 of these women were eventually reprieved. Of these, 27 had killed their own children.

Following the closure of Newgate, where execution of women prisoners had traditionally taken place, an execution shed was constructed at Holloway. Inside was the gallows, which had the capacity to hang two prisoners at the same time, side by side. Beneath the gallows was an empty cell that acted as the pit into which the hanged woman would drop when the trapdoor was released. Later, a fairly spacious condemned suite was built on the prison's first floor, consisting of five cells. One of these was a visiting cell in which a glass partition segregated the prisoner from visitors. There was also a bathroom and a day cell. The lights burned 24-hours a day and two wardresses kept a constant watch on the condemned woman.

The day cell had a wardrobe on one wall and this concealed the door that led through to the anteroom to the execution chamber. Executions always took place at 9am and afterwards bodies were removed to a cell adjacent to the 'drop' cell where a postmortem examination would be carried out. The women's bodies were then laid to rest in unmarked graves in the prison grounds at lunchtime on the same day.

Between 1903 and 1955 – the year that the hanging of women stopped, although it was not formally abolished for another ten years – five women were executed at Holloway. These included the last double hanging of women in the UK, that of Amelia Sach and Annie Walters, in 1903. They were convicted of 'baby farming'. This was the practice of taking in a child for payment, usually where it had been born out of wedlock. Sach offered her service for around £25 to £30 ($50 - $60) and her customers were most often servants who had been impregnated by their bosses. Unknown to her customers, however, once the babies had been delivered to Sach, they were collected by Walters, who poisoned them. Unfortunately, Walters' landlord happened to be a policeman and the pair were arrested after his suspicions had been aroused. Not before dozens of babies had died, however.

On 9 January, 1923, 20 years later, 28-year-old Edith Jessie Thompson was hanged at Holloway, exactly the same time as her lover Frederick Bywaters was meeting his maker at Pentonville Prison, just 0.8km (0.5 miles) away. She died, in spite of a clamour by the public for a reprieve, while another woman, 36-year-old Daisy Wright saw her sentence for the murder of her daughter commuted.

Another 18 women passed through Holloway's condemned cell during the next 21 years, all of them being reprieved. Then, in 1953, a 53-year-old Greek Cypriot woman, Styllou Pantopiou Christofi, arrived in the condemned suite.

Christofi had come to Britain to stay with her son, Stavros, who was working in Britain and had married a German girl, called Hella Bleicher. Unfortunately, Styllou and Hella never hit it off, and Styllou eventually hit her daughter-in-law on the head with a heavy ash pan and then strangled her, before setting fire to the body. The resulting fire got out of hand, however, and when the house threatened to burn down with her three grandchildren in it, Styllou had no alternative but to call for help. The police found the partly burned body of Hella in the kitchen and Styllou was convicted of murder and sentenced to death. She

ABOVE: 28-year-old Ruth Ellis, shown in a photo taken prior to her arrest for the murder of her lover, David Blakely.

was hung, by Albert Pierrepoint, on 13 December 1954.

After an absence of female executions for 21 years, until that of Styllou Christofi, another came along just seven months later. Ruth Ellis had fallen out with her boyfriend, David Blakely, over the Easter holiday and had lain in wait for him outside the Magdala public house in Hampstead. When he emerged, she pumped five bullets into him. After a huge public outcry, both in Britain and internationally, she was hanged on 13 July.

Although one more woman, Freda Rumbold, convicted of killing her husband, would spend time in the condemned cell at Holloway Prison, Ruth Ellis would be the last woman to be walk through the wardrobe on the wall of her cell to meet the hangman.

ALCATRAZ

SAN FRANCISCO BAY, USA

ALCATRAZ HAS PLAYED HOST TO SOME OF AMERICA'S MOST INFAMOUS CRIMINALS, INCLUDING GANGSTERS AL CAPONE AND ALVIN KARPIS. ALCATRAZ, OR 'THE ROCK', WAS PERFECTLY SUITED TO PURPOSE AS A HIGH-SECURITY PRISON. SURROUNDED BY TREACHEROUS, ICY-COLD WATERS AND MARAUDING SHARKS. LIFE INSIDE THE PRISON WAS TOUGH, BUT MANY OF THE CHALLENGES FACING AN ALCATRAZ ESCAPEE WERE FAR, FAR TOUGHER.

We know it simply as 'The Rock'. A small island in the middle of San Francisco Bay that was the toughest prison in the US from 1934 to 1963, a prison from which, it is claimed, no one ever escaped and lived to tell the tale. But when Alcatraz opened its doors, in 1934, to some 300 of the worst criminals in the US, it had already enjoyed a long and interesting history.

It was first visited by a European in 1775. Juan de Ayala, a naval officer on board the *San Carlos*, the first European ship to enter the bay, named the island '*La Isla de los Alcatraces*', which translated means 'Island of the Pelicans'. It was the discovery of gold in California and the start of the 'gold rush', in 1848, that really opened up the area and the bay was suddenly flooded with ships. The rocky Alcatraz was a danger to these ships and it was decided that the American west coast's first lighthouse should be built on the island. Its light was switched on for the first time in the summer of 1853. That lighthouse lasted until 1909, when a concrete tower with an automated rotating beacon replaced it.

Alcatraz was first owned, in 1846, by rancher Julian Workman, who was given the island by his friend, Pio Pico, the last Mexican governor of Alta California. Later that year, John C Fremont paid Workman $5,000 (£2,500) for it, and this was followed by a legal struggle during which the US wrestled control of the island. Following the Mexican-American War, and with the gold rush making California an attractive proposition, the island was fortified and a garrison was placed on it. The American Civil War saw it being used as a prison for Confederate sympathizers and its total suitability for this purpose – isolated with 1.6km (1 mile) of current-churned, icy water between it and the land – encouraged the US army to decide, in 1907, to designate Alcatraz as its western military prison. Construction on its large cellblock was begun and it opened for business in 1912, with a maximum capacity of 302.

It was a tough place to do time. Discipline was harsh and punishments for breaches of the rules were harsher. Hard labour awaited the wrongdoer and, in the worst cases, solitary confinement, with only bread and water to eat and drink. The inmates were mostly young men who were serving short sentences for desertion or more minor crimes. However, soldiers were incarcerated for longer for more serious crimes such as larceny, insubordination and even murder. Work duties depended on the nature of the prisoner. Some worked as cooks and cleaners for the families who lived on Alcatraz and, on the whole, the prison could be said to be minimum security at this time. Several inmates did try to escape, but it is believed that most of them died in the icy waters of the bay.

By the late 1920s, the prisoners had built a baseball field and, on Friday nights, the army staged what became known as 'Alcatraz Fights', boxing matches between inmates. The audiences for these bouts would include San Franciscans who had crossed to the island to see a good fight.

CENTRE LEFT: Police mug shot of Chicago mobster Al Capone.

CENTRE RIGHT: Alcatraz's longest serving prisoner: Alvin "Creepy" Karpis, shown here in a 1936 file photo.

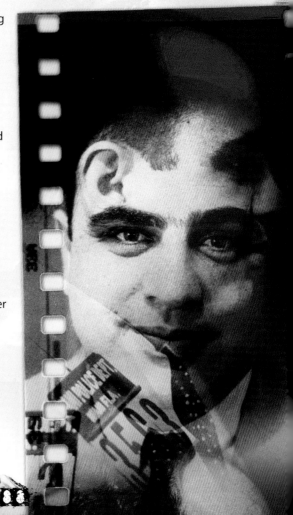

Prohibition and the poverty of the Depression had created an organized crime explosion on the streets of the US during the 1920s and attorney general Homer Cummings, did two things to fight the crime wave. First, in 1933, he created the Federal Bureau of Investigation (FBI). Second, he acquired Alcatraz from the army to use as a federal prison. It would be no ordinary prison, however. Robert Burge, one of America's top security experts, was brought in to design an escape-proof prison that also looked forbidding. Work began on upgrading the out-of-date old military facility. Modern tool-proof iron bars were put on all windows and doors, every cell was given an electricity supply. The tunnels carrying all the pipes and wires were filled with cement to prevent any prisoner from using them as an escape route, and special gun galleries surrounded the perimeters of the cellblock. These galleries were secure and out of reach of

the prisoners, allowing the guards to patrol carrying weapons. Tear-gas canisters in the roof of the dining hall could be released remotely and metal detectors were introduced in various locations. Outside, guard towers loomed over the prison.

Burge also designed the block so that its 350 cells were far from the perimeter wall. So, even if an inmate did succeed in burrowing out of his cell, freedom would still be some distance away.

The man chosen to run Alcatraz was James A Johnston, who had a humanistic approach to reform. During his 13 years in charge, he would eschew the customary barbaric methods used in prisons up to then, including the use of straitjackets for restraint and the punishment of solitary confinement in darkness. During spells as warden at both San Quentin and Folsom prisons, he had become distrustful of the use of chain gangs, but did believe that inmates should have a job from which they could earn respect as well as rewards.

However, life was still harsh for the inmates. They had to earn visitation rights and, indeed, they were not allowed visitors for their first three months on The Rock. Even when they were eventually allowed visitors, these were limited to just one a month. There was a prison library, but inmates were not allowed to have radios, newspapers or magazines. Mail was strictly controlled, it was considered a privilege that could be removed, and letters were carefully vetted before being sent or received. Above all, a good work detail had to be earned by good conduct.

Prisoners each had their own cell, but little else apart from the bare necessities – food, water, clothing and medical care should they need it. They were marched everywhere in formation and it did not take much for a privilege to be removed. Discipline was relentlessly applied, and it had to be.

Wardens of America's prisons were invited to send their worst inmates to Alcatraz, men who were inveterate escapers, or who had proved unmanageable. They were also asked to send high-profile prisoners who had been receiving special treatment because of who they were. No one received special treatment on The Rock.

Every day was the same. A roll call was taken at 6.30am. At 6.55am, the tiers of cells would be opened individually and the prisoners would march in line to the Mess Hall, where they would have 20 minutes to eat breakfast. They were then marched out to their work assignments.

Normally, in American prisons, the ratio of guards to prisoners was one guard for every 12 prisoners. In Alcatraz, however, it was one guard for every three prisoners and the guards carried out counts of the entire prison population no fewer than 12 times a day. The gun galleries ensured that inmates were under constant supervision and guards were also able to watch out for each other.

One of the harshest elements of warden Johnston's regime was his silence policy. Inmates were not allowed to talk to each other and only to guards when asked a question. It drove several inmates close to insanity and was the subject of much protest by the prisoners. It was later relaxed, to the great relief of the inmates.

The ultimate form of punishment was the Strip Cell, known by inmates as the 'Oriental'. It was a dark, steel-covered cell with no toilet or sink – merely a hole in the ground, the flushing of which was controlled by a guard. Inmates were put into the cell naked for two days and their diet was restricted. It was cold and there was no light. A mattress was only allowed at night.

There were 14 attempts to escape from Alcatraz between 1934 and 1963, involving 36 prisoners, two of whom were brave enough – or possibly stupid enough – to try twice. Seven were shot and killed, two drowned, five were unaccounted for, thought to have drowned in the bay's swirling waters, and the remainder were recaptured. Only two actually succeeded in reaching the mainland, but even they were recaptured.

On 11 June 1962, two brothers, John and Clarence Anglin and Frank Morris carried out one of Alcatraz's most daring escape attempts. They chiselled their way through the damp concrete around a steel grille, giving them access to a utility corridor that ran behind their cells. They contrived tools such as a metal spoon soldered with silver from a 10 cent coin and ingeniously constructed an electric drill using a stolen vacuum cleaner motor, the noise of which was hidden by accordions that were played during the prison music hour. The rivets from the grill were replaced by rivets fashioned from soap. They left dummies made from papier mâché and were in the bay by 10pm. They had stolen several raincoats from which they created a makeshift raft. Needless to say, articles relating to their escape were found washed up on a nearby island and the official report into the escape states that the three men drowned.

Alcatraz opened its doors to a number of infamous residents over the 29 years it served as a federal prison. Robert Stroud arrived there in 1942 and spent 17 years at Alcatraz for murder. He became famous as the Birdman of Alcatraz, taking solace from keeping birds in his cell. The most notorious gangster of them all, Al 'Scarface' Capone, arrived in 1934 after having received special treatment in his former prison in Atlanta, running his organisation while incarcerated and receiving special privileges by bribing guards. After four-and-a-half years, however, he began to show the debilitating effects of the syphilis, that would kill him a few years later, and was transferred to Terminal Island prison in Los Angeles. George 'Machine Gun' Kelly spent time there, as did several members of the Purple Gang, the leader of Boston's Winter Hill Gang, James 'Whitey' Bulger and Alvin Karpis, Public Enemy Number One and member of the murderous Karpis-Barker Gang during the 1930s. Karpis became Alcatraz's longest-serving inmate, spending more than 25 years there, from August 1936 until April 1962.

Alcatraz became prohibitively expensive to run, however. While at the start of the 1960s it cost $3 (£1.50) a day to keep a prisoner in an ordinary American institution, it cost almost $10 (£5.00) a day to keep a prisoner in Alcatraz. There was also a serious pollution danger posed by the sewage from the 250 prisoners and 60 families who lived on The Rock. A new prison to replace 'The Rock', was built at Marion in Illinois, and Alcatraz was closed for good on 21 March 1963.

OPPOSITE PAGE: A view of the solitary block at Alcatraz.

BELOW: Tags hang from the toes of dead Alcatraz escapees.

THE MANSON FAMILY

10050 CIELO DRIVE, LOS ANGELES, USA

CHARLES MANSON AND HIS 'FAMILY' HAVE GONE DOWN IN FOLK HISTORY AS THE MOST NOTORIOUS SERIAL KILLING CULTS OF ALL TIME, BUT THEY WERE LARGELY UNKNOWN UNTIL THE NIGHT OF 9 AUGUST 1969 – WHEN 'HELTER SKELTER' WAS UNLEASHED ON THE WEALTHY CELEBRITY INHABITANTS OF 10050 CIELO DRIVE. THE EXTRAORDINARILY VIOLENT EVENTS THAT TOOK PLACE THERE THAT NIGHT, MEANT THE WHOLE WORLD WOULD FIND OUT JUST WHO THE MANSON FAMILY WERE, AND WHAT THEY STOOD FOR.

10050 Cielo Drive was designed by Robert Byrd for the French actress Michèle Morgan, in 1944. This French country-style structure sat in 1.2 hectares (three acres) of land at the end of a cul-de-sac in Benedict canyon in the Santa Monica Mountains, west of Hollywood. Facing east and overlooking Beverly Hills and Bel Air, past residents had included Cary Grant and Dyan Cannon, Henry Fonda and record producer, Terry Melcher (son of Doris Day) and his girlfriend, Candice Bergen.

Charles Manson had spent more than half his 32 years in prison and institutions. In 1968, he was the leader of a group of hippies and drop-outs, called 'the Family' which had been living in the house of Beach Boy, Dennis Wilson. Wilson had expressed enthusiasm for some songs that Manson had written and introduced him to Terry Melcher at 10050 Cielo Drive. Melcher, however, was not as impressed as Wilson and decided he did not want to record Manson's songs. Eventually, Wilson and Melcher stopped taking his calls, and Manson was infuriated.

Not long after this, Melcher moved out of the Cielo Drive house, and it was rented by film director, Roman Polanski and his wife, Sharon Tate. Every so often, however, Manson would turn up at the house looking for Melcher, to be told, on more than one occasion, that he had moved.

Manson developed a strange philosophy that was partly based around the music of The Beatles. He assimilated their work, especially the newly released White Album into his belief that the blacks in America's cities would shortly rise up and slaughter the whites. He believed that The Beatles were talking directly to the Family through their lyrics.

In Topanga Canyon, he finessed his vision of the impending apocalypse, calling it 'Helter Skelter', after a track on the White Album. The Family would be safe while the killing was going on, he said; they would go into hiding in 'the bottomless pit', a secret city beneath Death Valley.

A few months later, on the night of 9 August 1969, Manson, having come to the conclusion that he would have to show the

BELOW: Clairvoyant Peter Hurkos studies the bloodstained living room where pregnant actress Sharon Tate and others were found murdered.

blacks the way, unleashed Helter Skelter. He ordered Family members, Charles 'Tex' Watson, Patricia Krenwinkel, Susan Atkins and Linda Kasabian to go to Cielo Drive and 'totally destroy everyone in it as gruesome as you can.'

Arriving at the quiet, secluded house, they cut the phone lines and climbed the fence into the grounds. A car approached and Watson instructed the girls to hide in some bushes. Pulling out a gun, he shot the car's driver dead. The young man in the car was eighteen-year-old Stephen Parent, who had been visiting William Garretson, a caretaker living in the guest house on the property. Watson then cut a hole in a screen at an open window and told Kasabian to wait at the gate. He and the two other girls climbed in through the window.

Wojciech Frykowski, a friend of Polanski, was sleeping on the sofa in the living room. 'I'm the devil, and I'm here to do the devil's business,' Watson chillingly announced. The other occupants of the house were rounded up: Tate, Jay Sebring, (America's top men's hair stylist) and twenty-five year-old Abigail Folger (a coffee heiress).

Watson tied Tate's and Sebring's necks together and threw the other end of the rope over a beam so that they would choke if they tried to escape. Watson then stabbed Folger several times. Frykowski freed his hands from the towel they had used to tie him up and tried to escape, but Watson shot him twice. At this point, Kasabian appeared, trying to bring a halt to proceedings, saying that someone was coming.

Folger, bleeding profusely, ran to the pool area where Krenwinkel and Watson stabbed her repeatedly. Frykowski was also stabbed by Watson while trying to crawl across the lawn. He was found later with 51 stab wounds to his body. Meanwhile, in the house, Sharon Tate was pleading for her life and that of her unborn baby. Atkins told her she did not care about her or her baby and she and Watson stabbed her 16 times.

Manson had asked them to leave a sign when they left. So, Atkins grabbed a towel and wrote the word 'pig' on the front door in Sharon Tate's blood.

The following night it was the turn of Leno LaBianca, a supermarket executive, and his wife, Rosemary, who were brutally murdered.

Eventually, it became clear that Charles Manson and his followers were connected to the killings and, in October, the desert ranches on which they were living were raided, and a couple of dozen people, including Manson, were arrested. Meanwhile, Susan Atkins confessed to detectives that she had been involved in the killing of a man called Gary Hinman. She also shared her story about the Sharon Tate murders with the women with whom she shared a cell.

Warrants were issued for Charles Watson, Patricia Krenwinkel and Linda Kasabian in the Tate case, and they were noted as suspects in the LaBianca case. Soon after, Kasabian had handed herself in to police, they were all under arrest. Kasabian had not taken part in the actual killings, and was granted immunity in exchange for testifying against the others.

The girls tried to twist their stories to take all the blame themselves and spare Charles, but, on 25 January, 1971, Manson, Krenwinkel and Atkins were found guilty of all seven charges of murder, and, Leslie Van Houten, who had been involved in the LaBianca murders, was found guilty of two counts of murder. Watson was found guilty on all seven counts later in the year. They were sentenced to death, but their sentences were commuted to life after the US supreme court declared the death penalty unconstitutional in 1972.

10050 Cielo Drive was occupied for a while by rock star Trent Reznor, of the band Nine Inch Nails, and was the site of sessions for his album Downward Spiral as well as sessions for Marilyn Manson's Reznor-produced Portrait of an American Family.

In 1994, the owner, American television producer, Jeff Franklin, demolished the house and built a new house called Villa Bella. It was allocated the new street address of 10066 Cielo Drive.

JONESTOWN
NORTHWESTERN GUYANA,
SOUTH AMERICA

REVEREND JIM JONES WAS A POWER-CRAZED LUNATIC, WHO CLAIMED, LIKE SO MANY OTHERS OF HIS ILK, THAT GOD WAS ON HIS SIDE. HE SUBJECTED HIS 'FOLLOWERS' TO MENTAL AND PHYSICAL TORTURE AT HIS JUNGLE HIDE-OUT IN GUYANA, AND KILLED THOSE WHO TRIED TO BREAK FREE. THE PEOPLE'S TEMPLE BECAME THE PEOPLE'S PRISON AND, ULTIMATELY, THE PEOPLE'S GRAVE.

Jim Jones called them 'White Nights'. His followers were ordered to line up. Then, when they had shuffled forward and arrived at the table, they would be given a small glass of red liquid to drink. They were informed that the liquid contained poison and that they would be dead within 45 minutes. However, when 45 minutes had passed, the Reverend Jones would explain that the poison was not actually real and that they had just been through a loyalty test. Chillingly, he would add that the time was approaching when it would not be a test – it would be necessary for them to take their own lives.

It was a grim dress rehearsal for what would occur on the night of 18th November 1978.

Jim Jones was born, in 1931, in Crete, Indiana and became obsessed with religion after finding it hard to make friends as a child. By 1947, aged just sixteen, he was preaching on street corners in both black and white neighbourhoods, sharing the wisdom and knowledge that he believed he possessed and was obliged to share with others. After selling pet monkeys door to door, to raise sufficient funds to start his own church, he founded Wings of Deliverance, later changing the name to the People's Temple. In 1964, his tiny church became affiliated with the Disciples of Christ, and Jones had access to a much larger congregation. His message became one of social justice and racial equality and this, coupled with the miracle healings he carried out during his sermons, helped to recruit many poor, uneducated Afro-Americans to his church. The People's Temple worked to feed the poor, find employment for the jobless and help ex-criminals and drug addicts put their lives back together. Many of these people, weak and disconnected from society would, in turn, become members of the church.

The People's Temple expanded, recruiting large numbers of new members and opening several churches and a headquarters in San Francisco. New recruits would find an organization based on brotherhood. They would witness Jones's miracle healings with putrid, cancerous tissue being 'torn' from people's insides and listen to his predictions. Little did

BELOW: Reverend Jim Jones and his wife, Marceline, taken from a pink photo album left behind in the village of the dead in Jonestown, Guyana.

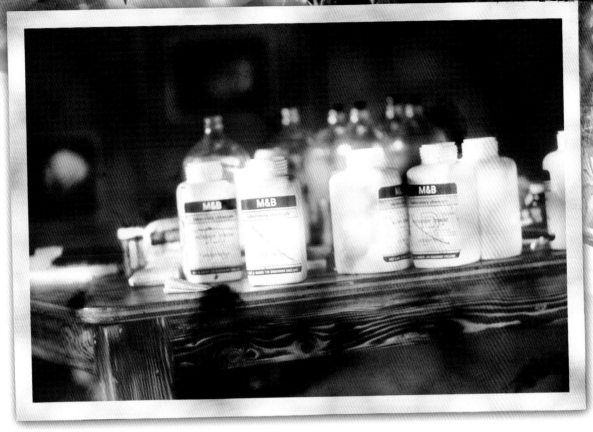

ABOVE: Bottles of cyanide as mixed with Kool-aid and ingested by members of the People's Temple.

they realize, however, that he had other members rifle through congregation members' rubbish to find out things about them that he could 'miraculously' surprise them with during his sermons.

Members had to undergo different levels of commitment until, eventually, they had given Jones everything – property, social-security payments and savings – and had renounced all outside ties. They could not leave because they, quite simply, had nowhere to go. They received room and board and a $2.00 (£1.00) a week allowance.

In Jones's eyes, this type of socialism or communalism was the manifestation of God. His miracles, healing of the sick and care for the poor were proof that he was, indeed, the living Christ.

Meanwhile, he would lecture his followers that the outside world was deeply suspicious of their success as a community and would try to destroy them. Defectors and dissidents were hated and any dissent from within was severely punished. If a member expressed doubts to anyone, even members of their own family, he or she was reported and punished. Children would

report on parents, husbands on wives and parents on their own children.

As tax officials closed in on Jones's activities, and the media became increasingly interested in his activities, his own paranoia became more extreme. Consequently, he concocted a plan to move the People's Temple to Guyana, in Central America. Proposing to create an agricultural utopia in the Guyanese jungle, far from racism and run on socialist principals, he bought 121 hectares (300 acres) of jungle from the Guyanese government. He built a township 225km (140 miles) from Georgetown which became home to around 900 Temple members. He called it Jonestown.

Jonestown, however, was no Shangri-la. The isolation was extreme, and armed guards patrolled its perimeters and the roads leading to the nearest town. Dissidents were unable to leave because they had no money and Jones held on to their passports. They had to work six days a week, from 7am until 6pm, in temperatures reaching more than 38°C (100°F). Meals were sparse, consisting mostly of rice and

ABOVE: The bodies of dead cult-members litter the sight of Jonestown, Guyana, 18 November, 1978.

worked hard to persuade the visitors that all was well and everyone was happy at Jonestown.

At some point in the evening, however, Ryan was slipped a note written by a couple of Temple members, Vernon Gosney and Monica Bagby. The note read, 'Dear Congressman … Please help us get out of Jonestown.'

More announced they wanted to defect and by the time the party was due to leave, on 18 November, 15 had volunteered. Jones reluctantly gave them permission – worrying that they would spread poisonous stories about Jonestown – and issued them with passports and some money. Ryan, wishing to remain behind to see what else was to be done, was finally dissuaded when a Temple member attacked him with a knife, probably under orders from Jones. The party nervously set off for the Port Kaituma airstrip, where two planes would be readied to take them home.

The first of them boarded the Cessna and, at around 5.10pm, as it was preparing for take-off, a passenger, Larry Layton, a

beans, while Jones, himself, enjoyed eggs, meat, fruit and salads. There was also a great deal of sickness.

Punishments were often harsh. Jones ordered beatings and imprisoned wrongdoers in a tiny plywood box. There was also a well at the bottom of which children were occasionally forced to spend the night, sometimes hanging upside down.

Jones was universally addressed as 'Father' or 'Dad', and was bringing in up to $65,000 (£32,500.00) a month in social-security payments. It was estimated that he was worth at least $26 million (£13 million).

Congressman Leo Ryan had long been interested in Jones's church and, on 14 November 1978, he flew, with a party of government officials, media representatives and concerned relatives of Temple members, to Guyana to investigate what was happening. They were at first refused entry to the compound, but Jones relented and they spent an evening there being entertained by Temple members. Jones

Jones loyalist who had surprised everyone with his desire to leave Jonestown, pulled a gun and opened fire on the other passengers. He wounded Monica Bagby and Vernon Gosney and tried to kill another man, who succeeded in disarming him.

At the same time, however, a wagon pulled by a tractor pulled up at the airport. It was filled with Jones's armed guards who opened fire on the other plane, a Twin Otter, and its passengers who were on the tarmac preparing to board. Congressman Ryan; NBC cameraman, Bob Brown; reporters Greg Robinson and Don Harris and, defector, Patricia Parks, all died in a hail of bullets. Nine others were injured. The majority of the survivors clambered aboard the Cessna and flew out, while a few remained behind to tend to the injured.

Meanwhile, back at Jonestown, another 'White Night' was staged, but this time the soft drink was laced with diazepam, chloral hydrate, and, probably, cyanide.

Jones had called everyone to a meeting around the time the shooting was breaking out at the airfield. 'One of the people on that plane, is gonna shoot the pilot, I know that, he told them. 'I didn't plan it but I know it's going to happen. They're gonna shoot that pilot and down comes the plane into the jungle and we had better not have any of our children left when it's over, because they'll parachute in here on us... They'll torture our children,' he continued. They'll torture some of our people here, they'll torture our seniors. We cannot have this.' As for dying, he said, 'All it is, is taking a drink to take... to go to sleep. That's what death is, sleep.'

They poisoned the children first, spraying the liquid into their mouths using syringes, and then moved on to the adults. It was very effective and death followed after only around five minutes.

Finally, Jones and his immediate supporters came together, gave a final cheer and shot each other with handguns. Jim Jones was found seated in a deckchair with a gunshot wound to the head.

Around him, dead, lay 913 members of the People's Temple.

BELOW: The bloated body of Reverend Jim Jones lies on the ground on 18 November, 1978, after officials have conducted a hasty autopsy and sewn it back up.

THE CURSE OF PEARL BRYAN

44 LICKING PIKE,
WILDER, KENTUCKY, USA

LOCALS AND PSYCHIC INVESTIGATORS HAVE OFTEN REFERRED TO BOBBY MACKEY'S MUSIC WORLD IN WILDER, KENTUCKY, AS 'HELL'S GATE', DUE TO THE SHEER STRENGTH OF THE MALEVOLENT PARANORMAL FORCES AT WORK THERE. ITS FASCINATING HISTORY BEGAN WITH THE VICIOUS MURDER OF PEARL BRYAN. THE CURSE HER MURDERERS PLACED ON THE BUILDING IS STILL GOING STRONG OVER A CENTURY LATER.

THE CORONER PULLED THE DRESS DOWN AND WAS HORRIFIED TO FIND THAT SHE HAD NO HEAD.

Bobby Mackey purchased the club that bears his name – Bobby Mackey's Music World – in 1978. Located in Wilder, Kentucky, it occupies the site of a former slaughterhouse. The music at Bobby Mackey's is country, and it even boasts a mechanical bull for those brave enough. It has become more famous as home of numerous ghosts, the most famous of which is that of Pearl Bryan, victim of one of the most infamous crimes in Kentucky's history.

Pearl, a pretty, auburn-haired 22-year-old Greencastle, Indiana woman, who was the daughter of a wealthy farmer, travelled to Cincinnati, in 1896, with a secret. She was pregnant. The father was a young dental student, 28-year-old Scott Jackson, who had met Pearl while paying a visit to his mother in Greencastle. He liked the sociable, unspoilt country girl and they became friends. When she realized she was pregnant, she confided in a cousin, who wrote to Jackson. He told Pearl to come to Cincinnati and her train pulled into the city's station on the night of 28 January.

Waiting for her was Jackson – 1m 68cm (5ft 6 ins) tall, with blond hair and cold, grey eyes, and his friend, dark-haired fellow dental student, Alonzo Walling. The three headed downtown and were overheard engaged in an argument. They then went to Legner's Tavern, where the two men apparently put cocaine into the sarsaparilla Pearl was drinking.

The group were picked up by a coachman, who took them through Newport and into Wilder, then to Alexandria Pike and into Fort Thomas. The coachman dropped them off on a side road and returned to Cincinnati.

A couple of days later, a man called John Hewing was taking a shortcut across a field on his way to work, when he saw a woman lying on the ground. It was not that unusual a sight as soldiers from a nearby army post were in the habit of bringing women out to this area. Sometimes the women were very drunk and, at first, that is what Hewison presumed.

Arriving at work, he mentioned her to his employer and the deputy sheriff was summoned. When he arrived, accompanied by the coroner, he noticed signs of a struggle. Her dress was pulled up over her head and there was a pool of blood at her feet. The coroner pulled the dress down and was horrified to find that she had no head. She had been decapitated.

Thinking the head must be nearby, they searched the surrounding area, bringing in bloodhounds. However, there was still no sign of it. They even had a nearby reservoir drained, but were still unable to find it.

The autopsy concluded that the woman had been pregnant and traces of cocaine were found in her stomach. Eventually, they identified her by tracing back a manufacturer's number in her shoes.

When Pearl's family were informed, her cousin volunteered the information that he had written to Scott Jackson, explaining her predicament, and that Jackson had suggested she come to Cincinnati. Jackson was picked up that same evening and Alonzo Walling was arrested the following day, after Jackson accused him of carrying out the murder. Needless to say, Walling accused his friend, saying that he had been asked to perform an abortion on Pearl, but then Jackson had suggested that they poison her and make it look like she had committed suicide.

The two were charged with murder, and the police pursued the matter of what had become of Pearl's head. They brought in her sister to try to persuade them to tell them of the head's location, but Jackson and Walling were unwavering in their desire to keep it secret.

When Jackson was tried, his case was not helped when it emerged that Pearl may have been alive when they began to decapitate her and, after 23 days in court, he was found guilty and sentenced to death by hanging. Walling received the same sentence.

Meanwhile, the public had become incensed by the case, and the two men had to be heavily guarded in case there was an attempt to lynch them. Even when there was a prison break the two remained in their cells, because it was safer for them there than on the outside.

On the day of their hanging, a huge crowd gathered. Three minutes before the time of the hanging, Scott Jackson asked to speak to the chaplain and then let it be known that he wanted to make a statement about Walling. 'I know that Alonzo M Walling is not guilty of murder,' he said to a stunned audience.

The prison authorities telegraphed the state governor, William Bradley. He asked for more information from Jackson, but ,when Jackson was questioned once more, he said he had nothing to add to what he had already said. More than 2.5 hours after they had originally been due to hang, they walked out to the gallows.

They were a contrasting pair: Jackson erect and confident, Walling agitated and downcast. When asked if he had anything further to say, Jackson thought long and hard. Walling turned towards him expectantly, hoping that his friend would say something that would save him. He was devastated, however, when Jackson merely said, 'I have only this to say, that I am not guilty of the crime for which I am now compelled to pay the penalty of my life.'

Walling, asked if he had anything to say, replied, 'Nothing, only that you are taking the life of an innocent man and I will call upon God to witness the truth of what I say.'

At 11.40am the trapdoor opened and the two men were dispatched.

Legend has it that the murderers cursed Pearl's head and the area in which she was killed. It is thought that the head may have been used in a satanic ritual and thrown down an old well situated in the basement of a slaughterhouse that was in use until the early 1890s. Some say that the well is a portal for demons and locals dubbed it 'Hell's Gate'.

The basement is said to have been a venue for the activities of local occultists practicing satanic rites and that Jackson and Walling were afraid of upsetting the Satanists and bringing the wrath of Satan down upon themselves if they revealed the whereabouts of the head. As the noose was being slipped over his head, Walling stated that he would come back and haunt the area, and it is also suggested that many of the people involved in the case later met with bad luck and tragic deaths.

Now Bobby Mackey's is said to be filled, nightly, with ghostly mutterings, lights switching on and off, a dark, very angry young man and a headless woman wearing 19th century clothing.

BELOW: Scot Jackson and Alonzo Walling, the killers of Pearl Bryan, are executed for her murder.

WONDERLAND MURDERS

8673 WONDERLAND,
LOS ANGELES, USA

8673 WONDERLAND WAS WELL-KNOWN TO THE LAPD DURING THE EARLY 1980S. IT WAS A BUSY DRUG DEN, WHERE PEOPLE FROM ALL WALKS-OF-LIFE CAME TO BUY COCAINE, HEROIN, OR WHATEVER THEY NEEDED TO GET THROUGH THE DAY. ON 1 JULY 1981 THE WONDERLAND PARTY CAME TO AN ABRUPT END, WHEN FOUR PEOPLE WERE SAVAGELY BLUDGEONED TO DEATH AS THEY SLEPT.

Laurel Canyon, in Los Angeles, consists of one main thoroughfare, Laurel Canyon Boulevard, which stretches up to Mulholland Drive with side streets, mainly cul-de-sacs, leading off it. It has been the home to countless celebrities over the years, from silent film star, Tom Mix, to Harry Houdini, Frank Zappa, The Byrds, Buffalo Springfield and Joni Mitchell, whose third album, *Ladies of the Canyon*, was inspired by the area.

But Laurel Canyon was also the setting for one of America's most gruesome killings, the incident known as the Wonderland Murders, aka the Four on the Floor or Laurel Canyon Murders.

8673 Wonderland Avenue is a white, stucco, two-storey building. These days, it is quiet and unremarkable, but, in the early 1980s, passers by would have remarked upon the metal cage that encased the stairway leading to the front door. The two vicious-looking pit bull terriers that patrolled the cage's interior would have made anyone take a cautious step back. Inside, the inhabitants of 8673 Wonderland Avenue were a no-less vicious bunch.

Ron Launius was the Wonderland Gang's leader. He had served in Vietnam

OPPOSITE PAGE: Porn star John Holmes is escorted to a waiting police van, after appearing before a County Municipal Court, in Los Angeles, on 9 December, 1981.

but, by the time of his death, he was being investigated for 27 murders, many of them witnesses who would testify against him on previous murders. He was a ruthless, violent killer who took drugs to excess, as well as dealing in them.

Billy Deverell was Launius's lieutenant and a heroin user who often expressed a desire to make a fresh start. He was often the voice of reason in the face of Launius's irrationality.

David Lind was a member of the white suprematist group, the Aryan Brotherhood, a member of a biker gang and a junkie. When Launius got to know Lind in prison, he persuaded him to become his partner in a drug-running operation. His criminal record included burglary, forgery, assault and attempted rape.

Billy Deverell's girlfriend, Joy Audrey Gold Miller, was a divorced mother whose children were grown up. She was a junkie and her habit saw her introduced to the Wonderland Gang. She was the actual tenant of the Wonderland house.

The house was a pharmacy where you could obtain almost any drug – cocaine, heroin, uppers and downers. All sorts of people, from rock stars to drop-outs, visited, day or night, to pick up their requirements, and rock music blasted the neighbourhood 24 hours a day.

There was also a thriving trade in stolen property at 8673 Wonderland Avenue, much of it provided by John Holmes. Holmes was an extraordinary character, a porn star who had reached the heights of his profession because he was the proud owner of a 30cm (12 in) penis. He had made a series of films in which he starred as Johnny Wadd, a private detective whose escapades did not just involve solving crimes. He claimed to have made 2,000 porn films and to have earned $6,000 (£3,000) a day doing so. He also calculated that he had slept with around 14,000 women. Unfortunately, however, by the late 1970s, Holmes had developed a huge cocaine habit and producers had stopped calling as his body began to display the ravages caused by excess. He now fed his habit by stealing luggage at Los Angeles airport and breaking into cars.

Holmes became the go-between for a powerful Los Angeles drug dealer, Eddie Nash and the Wonderland crew. Items stolen by Holmes and the others were paid for by Nash in drugs.

The Wonderland Gang were aware that Nash kept large supplies of drugs and cash at his mansion and, in, 1981, they decided to break in and steal his stash.

On 29 June, Launius, Lind and Deverell entered the house through a sliding glass door that had been surreptitiously unlocked by John Holmes on a recent visit. Encountering Nash's 300lb (136kg) bodyguard, Lind pulled out a forged LAPD badge and told the man he was under arrest. As Lind handcuffed him, his gun accidentally discharged, grazing the bodyguard's side. Hearing the sound, Nash came running in, wearing his customary brightly coloured bikini briefs, and threw himself on their mercy, pleading not to be killed.

They forced him to open his safe, which contained almost $200,000 (£100,000) as well as substantial quantities of heroin, cocaine, methaqualone and jewellery, a haul estimated to be worth around $1 million (£500,000).

The Wonderland boys grabbed the lot and drove back to their house, elated. Nash,

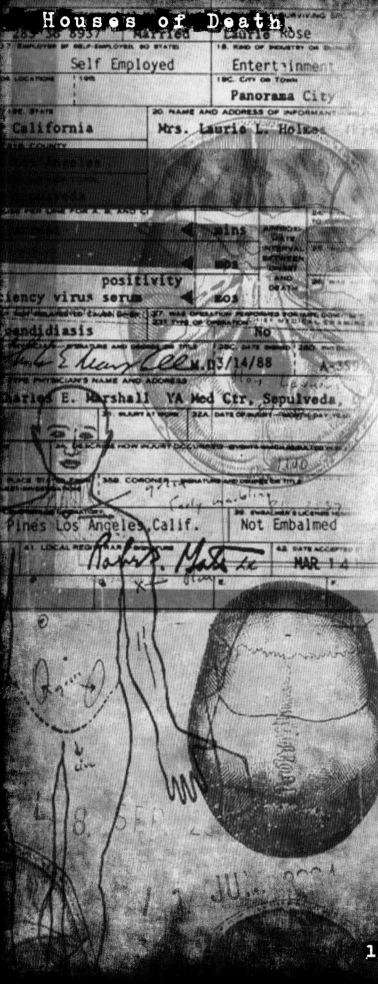

on the other hand, was furious at not only being robbed, but also being humiliated. He swore revenge.

A little over a day later, at 4am on 1 July, three men crept towards 8673 Wonderland Avenue, carrying heavy-duty lead pipes. They entered the house and then crept from bedroom to bedroom, bludgeoning the occupants with the pipes, killing four and critically injuring one. It was a bloodbath. Blood dripped from the walls, and the victims, their faces caved in, were no longer recognizable.

On hearing the uproar, neighbours thought it was just another night at the drug den. They drew their curtains and went back to bed or turned their televisions up loud to drown out the noise.

The mayhem was discovered the next day. Twelve hours after the onslaught, a removal man working in the adjoining house, heard groans coming from 8673 and could hardly fail to hear the dogs' continuous barking. The door was ajar and he went in to find a gruesome scene. Barbara Richardson, a friend of Lind, was lying on a sofa in the living room; Joy Miller was sprawled on a bed and Billy Deverell's blood-soaked body lay in the same room. Ron Launius was in a bedroom on the first floor and, beside him lay his wife, Susan, so seriously injured that surgeons had to later remove part of her skull. The floors of the house were swimming in blood.

David Lind had been lucky, having spent the night in a motel with a prostitute. When the police found him, he told them about the Nash robbery and about John Holmes. The police were anxious to locate Holmes to learn whether he had been involved especially as Lind told them that Holmes had been particularly unhappy about his share of the Nash robbery haul.

Holmes had arrived at his wife's house several hours after the Wonderland killings, his clothes soaked in blood. He had a shower and then took off with his young mistress, Diane Schiller. Nine days later, he was arrested in a motel in Sherman Oaks in the San Fernando Valley. Freed after questioning, but warned not to leave town,

Holmes again went to his wife's house where, she later claimed, he confessed to his involvement in the murders. He told her that he had been spotted by an associate of Nash, wearing a piece of jewellery that had been taken from the safe at Nash's house. He was taken to Nash and threatened that if he did not take them to the men who had committed the robbery, his family would be harmed. He told her he took them to Wonderland Avenue and watched as they bashed in the skulls of the occupants. In his autobiography, however, Holmes discounts this version of events, claiming that he was actually held captive at Nash's house while the killings were carried out.

Nonetheless, he was formally charged with the murders in December 1981. The main piece of evidence was a bloody palm-print belonging to him that was found on the rail of Launius's bed. However, the jury bought Holmes's assertion that he had been forced to watch the carnage at gunpoint and he was acquitted. When he refused to testify before a Los Angeles County Grand Jury however, he went to jail, for 110 days. There, he claimed his warders would watch him as he showered, amazed at his physical peculiarity. Holmes died of AIDS in 1988, not long after marrying his second wife, the porn star, Misty Dawn.

A few months after Holmes's death, Eddie Nash and his bodyguard, Gregory DeWitt Diles, were charged with the Wonderland murders. The sensation of this case was the prosecution's star witness, Scott Thorson, boyfriend of the piano-playing mega-celebrity, Liberace. Thorson said he had been present on the night Nash had threatened Holmes. He described how Nash had thrown Holmes against the wall and threatened him.

The jury could not come to a verdict and, at a retrial the following year, Nash was acquitted.

Finally, in 2001, after being hounded by the authorities for years, Nash confessed. Then 72 years old, and not a well man, he faced charges of racketeering as well as the Wonderland killings. He had already been acquitted of the murder charges and the best the prosecution could do was charge him with conspiracy to murder. He went to prison for only 37 months.

John Holmes had been concerned as he approached death that someone would snip off his famous penis. He instructed his wife to inspect his body before it was cremated to ensure it was intact. She reported that everything was as it should be.

BELOW: Porn star John Holmes speaks to the press shortly after his release from Los Angeles County Jail, on November 22, 1982.

WAVERLY HILLS SANATORIUM

LOUISVILLE, KENTUCKY, USA

MANY PEOPLE WHO ENTERED WAVERLY HILLS SANATORIUM LEFT VIA THE 'BODY CHUTE', A TUNNEL WITH A MOTORIZED RAIL AND CABLE SYSTEM SET UP TO TRANSPORT DISEASE-RIDDEN CORPSES AWAY FROM THE WARDS AND DOWN TO THE RAILWAY TRACKS AS QUICKLY AND AS EFFICIENTLY AS POSSIBLE. THE WAVERLY WAS REGARDED AS THE PLACE TO COME FOR THE TREATMENT OF TUBERCULOSIS, BUT DURING THESE PRIMITIVE TIMES, SOME OF THE EXPERIMENTS PRACTISED ON PATIENTS, IN THE NAME OF MEDICAL RESEARCH, LEFT A LOT TO BE DESIRED.

It is believed to be one of the most paranormally active locations in the entire world, and no wonder, for it is estimated that up to 63,000 people have died there during the last 100 years.

It started out innocently enough when, in 1883, Major Thomas Hays purchased some land on which to build a home for his family. As the house was far from the nearest school, Major Hays decided to open his own one-room schoolhouse. The teacher named it Waverly School and the major, liking the name, called his property Waverly Hills.

The low valley and swampland, in which Louisville is located, provided the perfect breeding ground for the disease known as the 'White Death', the dreaded, deadly and infectious killer, tuberculosis, that ravaged the US during the early years of its history. Louisville had the highest death rate from tuberculosis in the US and it badly needed hospitals in which to care for the sick. In 1924, $11 million was raised to build a Tuberculosis hospital. Waverly Hills Hospital opened its doors in 1926.

Waverly Hills was, at the time, the most advanced hospital for the treatment of tuberculosis in the country, but treatment was still fairly primitive. Nutritious food, rest and fresh air were considered the best treatments, but they were fighting a losing battle – at the height of the epidemic, patients were dying at the rate of one an hour.

It was not only the patients who died. Doctors and nurses also lost their lives treating patients or trying to find a cure. They carried out experiments, some barbaric and some effective. They would expose the lungs to ultraviolet light in 'sun rooms' in an effort to prevent the spread of bacteria. Or patients were placed in the open air on roofs or terraces, regardless of the weather, to take in air and be exposed to sunlight. There are pictures of patients who are dying, covered in snow.

There were more invasive experiments. Balloons would be inserted surgically into the lungs and filled with air to try to expand the lungs. Hydrotherapy was tried and resulted in the deaths of patients from pneumonia. In one procedure, the chest of the patient was opened and muscle and ribs were removed to allow the lungs more room in which to expand. Needless to say, this was often carried out when all else had failed. Fewer than 5% of patients undergoing this operation survived.

The huge numbers of dead left Waverly Hills through a corridor known as the 'body chute', a tunnel that led from the hospital down to a railway line at the bottom of the hill on which the hospital stood. It had a motorized rail and cable system by means of which bodies were lowered down one side of the tunnel. On the other were steps leading back up to the hospital. The tunnel was totally enclosed so that patients could not see how many bodies were leaving the institution.

In 1943, Albert Schatz, a young, graduate student at Rutgers University in New Jersey, discovered streptomycin, and tuberculosis was finally beaten. As numbers of victims fell, Waverly Hills became redundant,

There are pictures of patients who are dying, covered in snow

closing in 1961 and reopening as Woodhaven Geriatrics Sanatorium, in 1962.

Its new guise did not lessen the horrors of the place, however, and rumours of mistreatment and bizarre experiments persisted over the years, as they did in many such institutions. In those days, electroshock therapy was a widely used treatment for the mentally ill, often resulting in tragic losses.

Finally, in 1982, the state of Kentucky had had enough of the patient abuse, and Woodhaven was closed down. The land and the building and its contents were auctioned off.

The bizarre history of this eerie place was far from over, however. It changed hands a number of times over the next 18 years. One of the owners bought it with the intention of tearing the buildings down and, on the hill they occupied, to build the world's largest statue of Jesus Christ. Having demolished all the buildings apart from the main hospital, he was stopped only by an injunction from tearing that

down. Waverly Hills was finally registered on the National Historic Register's list of endangered buildings and could not be demolished. The owner then tried to make it fall down, inviting vandals in to smash windows, toilets, sinks and doors. He then dug around the foundations, sometimes to a depth of 30 feet to try to bring it down, but the old building withstood his attacks.

Waverly Hills, the ultimate house of death, is now a ramshackle ruin, but it is a major destination for ghost hunters. Stories abound of ghostly happenings – a little girl who plays hide and seek with trespassers, a little boy who plays with a ball, rooms lighting up even though the place has had no power for decades. Doors slam, disembodied voices plead with visitors to go away, a hearse has been seen delivering coffins, an old woman is often seen running from the front entrance with blood pouring from her wrists, screaming, 'Help me! Somebody save me!'

At Waverly Hills, 63,000 ghosts are ready to give visitors a chilly welcome.

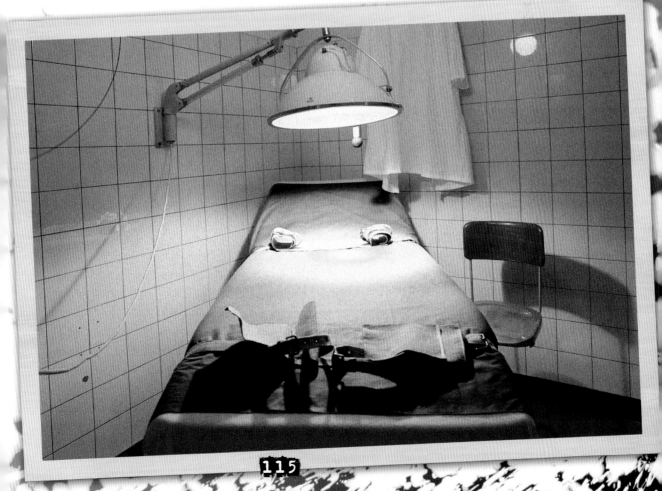

GAMBINO
MAFIA FAMILY

THE GEMINI LOUNGE,
BROOKLYN, USA

THE GEMINI LOUNGE IN BROOKLYN, NEW YORK, WAS A 'CHOP HOUSE' FOR THE GAMBINO MAFIA FAMILY FROM THE MID 1970S TO THE EARLY 1980S. CONTRACTS WERE LURED THERE WITH THE PROMISE OF WINE, WOMEN AND SONG, ONLY TO BE SHOT, STABBED AND DISMEMBERED IN THE APARTMENT UPSTAIRS. TODAY THE SPACE THAT WAS LEFT BY THE GEMINI LOUNGE HAS BEEN FILLED BY A SHOP-FRONT CHURCH CALLED FLATLANDS CHURCH - A HOUSE OF THE MOB HAS BECOME A HOUSE OF GOD.

Phil's Bar, later known as the Gemini Lounge, occupied the front half of a two-storey building located on a street corner in Flatlands, Brooklyn. In 1965, Roy DeMeo, who had been using it anyway to do business – loan-sharking, fencing stolen goods – bought into the bar.

DeMeo had been born in the neighbourhood, in 1940, to hard-working Italian immigrants who had come to New York to escape the grinding poverty of southern Italy. Young Roy had started learning early. His neighbour was Mafia boss Joe Profaci, and Profaci's sons taught him all there was to know about loan-sharking. By seventeen, it was a full-time occupation for him and he had no qualms about using a little 'persuasion' to make his borrowers pay up in time. As he got older, he married and prospered. He finally gave up his day job at a local supermarket and became a professional criminal.

DeMeo had been on the edges of the Lucchese Crime Family for a number of years when he made the acquaintance of Anthony 'Nino' Gaggi, a lieutenant in the Gambino family. By now, he was into car theft and trafficking drugs – dealing cocaine out of the Gemini Lounge – and had surrounded himself with a bunch of social misfits and killers. Among these were Harvey 'Chris' Rosenberg, a friend who had been dealing drugs using funds provided by the young DeMeo; Joey 'Dracula' Gugliemo, DeMeo's cousin, a pornographer and killer whose strange practices with the blood of victims in the rooms behind the Gemini Lounge earned him his chilling nickname; Joseph Testa and Anthony Senter, who were known as the Gemini Twins because they were inseparable and could always be found in the Gemini Lounge, and Joey's younger brother, Patrick Testa.

DeMeo was a late developer in the area of murder; he was 32 when he carried out his first, killing his colleague, Chris Rothenberg, outside a diner after Nino Gaggi had claimed he was about to cooperate with the police. DeMeo pumped two bullets into Rothenberg's head in an alleyway.

Other killings followed. Andrei Katz, who ran a car bodyshop in Flatlands, was also suspected of being an informer. He was lured to an apartment by a woman, abducted by DeMeo's men and taken to the meat department of a local supermarket, where he was dismembered by DeMeo and Joey Testa, who had both been apprenticed as butchers in their youth. He was decapitated and his head was crushed in a machine used for compacting cardboard. On another occasion, he and Gaggi flew to Florida to kill George Byrum who had been involved in a robbery at Gaggi's house. They shot him in DeMeo's hotel room, but fled, leaving the body in the bath, its head half sawn off.

By 1978, DeMeo was claiming to have committed 100 murders, and he let it be known that he and his crew were open to contracts. They carried out several for as little as $5,000 (£2,500). Some were even done for free – 'personal favour', he would say.

The preferred method was to lure the intended victim to the Gemini Lounge and ply him with booze. When he was sufficiently relaxed, he would be enticed through the side door and into the apartment that abutted the building at the back with a game of poker, some easy women or, perhaps, a nice meal.

Once there, someone would approach him from behind, carrying a gun fitted with a silencer in one hand. In the other hand he held a towel. He would fire a bullet into the victim's head, but moved swiftly to wrap the towel around the wound in order to stop the flow of blood and the resulting mess. Then, an accomplice would stab the victim through the heart with a sharp knife, ensuring that he severed arteries and prevented blood from being pumped around the body and eventually out of the head wound.

LEFT: Anthony 'Nino' Gaggi.

Reassured that their victim was dead, the Gemini Crew would then undress him and carry him into the bathroom. There, they would hang him upside down over the bath to let all the blood drain out of his body. The body was then carried into the living room and placed on a large pool liner. At that point, DeMeo and Joey Testa's butchery skills again came in handy, as the body was dismembered and all the parts were sealed in separate bags which were then placed in boxes and sent to the Fountain Avenue Dump, in Brooklyn, never to be seen again. It became known as the Gemini Method.

**FRED &
ROSE WEST**

25 CROMWELL STREET,
GLOUCESTER, ENGLAND

THE NOW-FAMOUS PICTURES TAKEN BY
JOURNALISTS OF THE POLICE SEARCH
AT 25 CROMWELL STREET WILL BE
FOREVER EMBLAZONED ON BRITISH
MEMORIES. THEY SERVE AS A STARK
REMINDER OF WHAT CAN HAPPEN WHEN
SOCIETY TURNS ITS BACK ON A FAMILY
IN TROUBLE. A TOTAL OF 12 YOUNG
WOMEN WERE RAPED, TORTURED AND
EVENTUALLY KILLED BY FRED AND ROSE
WEST, INCLUDING TWO OF THEIR OWN
DAUGHTERS. IT IS INCREDIBLE TO THINK
THAT NOBODY NOTICED THESE YOUNG
WOMEN VANISHING, ONE BY ONE, FROM
25 CROMWELL STREET.

It was an ordinary three-storey house situated near the centre of the attractive cathedral city of Gloucester. But 25 Cromwell Street was no ordinary house. It was a house where young women came to stay or visit and were never seen again, a house where even its young occupants were not safe from the voracious and depraved sexual appetites of its two owners – Fred and Rosemary West.

Fred and Rose were made for each other, both coming from dysfunctional, poor and possibly abusive backgrounds. Fred claimed, although it was never proven, that his father had sexually assaulted his own daughters, and Fred grew up with the attitude that girls and women were on this earth for one reason only – to satisfy his sexual needs. Rose was the daughter of a mother who suffered from severe depression and a father who was a schizophrenic, a violent and predatory domestic tyrant who demanded total

obedience and used extreme violence to obtain it. He was also said to molest young girls and unsubstantiated reports suggest he indulged in an incestuous relationship with his overweight and backward daughter, Rose.

By the time Fred and Rose met, he had been involved in petty crime and had got a 13-year-old girl, a friend of the family, pregnant. He was thrown out of the family house but escaped with a non-custodial sentence.

Fred fell for a young Scottish girl, Rena Costello, an occasional prostitute, who was pregnant with the child of an Asian bus driver. The two moved to Scotland where they married, and baby Charmaine was born. She was followed in 1964 by a child by Fred – Anna Marie. Fred earned a living driving an ice cream van, a job that drew countless young girls into his circle. When he accidentally ran over and killed a young boy, however, the couple moved back to

BELOW: Police search for bodies in the garden of 25 Cromwell Street.

Gloucester, accompanied by a woman called Anna McFall, whom they had befriended.

Fred found work in a local slaughterhouse, a job that would, chillingly, be useful to him later. By this time, his relationship with Rena was beginning to fall apart, and she returned to Scotland, without the children, returning in July 1966. Fred was now living in a caravan with McFall. His sexual appetite, however, was undiminished and it is not entirely coincidental that around this time in Gloucester there were eight sexual assaults committed by a man resembling Fred.

Anna McFall was pregnant with Fred's baby and keen for Fred to divorce Rena and marry her. Instead, Fred killed her, dismembering her body and cutting off her fingers and toes, which he buried separately, a signature feature of many of his murders. Rena moved back in with him and went to work on the streets. Fred, meanwhile, was unashamedly assaulting her daughter Charmaine in front of her.

Mary Bastholme was an attractive 15-year-old, who was on her way to play

ABOVE: Heather West.

Fred and Rose now had an even greater bond between them – MURDER

Monopoly at a friend's house when she disappeared in January 1968. Fred abducted her from the bus stop where she was waiting, leaving only a few pieces of the game behind, scattered on the pavement. Abducting girls from bus stops would later become one of Fred's favourite pastimes.

On 29 November 1968, Fred was working as a bakery delivery driver. That day he met the woman who was to become his partner in some of the most horrific crimes Britain has ever seen, 15-year-old Rosemary Letts.

Some months later, aged sixteen, Rose Letts left home and moved in with West, taking care of the children while he went to prison for theft. In 1970, she gave birth to Fred's daughter, Heather.

Rose was now looking after three children on her own while Fred was incarcerated, and her treatment of them – especially of the two who were not hers

– was appalling. In the summer of 1971, she murdered Rena's child, Charmaine, explaining her disappearance by telling people that Rena had come back and taken the child away. Fred was in jail at the time, but when he came home, he buried Charmaine's body under the kitchen floor of the house in which they were living, in Midland Road.

Fred and Rose now had an even greater bond between them – murder.

Of course, there was always the chance that Rena would come looking for her child, and she did, in August 1971. Fred took care of the problem by strangling Rena. He dismembered her, again cutting off the fingers and toes, and buried her locally.

Following the birth of another child, Mae, Fred and Rose married, in June 1972. They then moved their growing family into a larger house. It was semi-detached with a garage and a cellar which might come in useful for Rose's prostitution business, or, as Fred jokingly told a neighbor, as a soundproof torture chamber. It was big enough to allow them to take in lodgers to pay the rent on the property. The address was 25 Cromwell Street.

The first visitor to the cellar was Anna Marie, Fred's child with Anna McFall, who was raped by her father, while being held down by Rose. She was told that it was to enable her to learn how to satisfy a husband when she eventually married. The rapes became routine and she was threatened with beatings if she told anyone.

Attractive 17 year-old Caroline Owens became nanny to the Wests in late 1972, after Fred had picked her up. Trying to leave after both Fred and Rose had tried to seduce her, she was stripped and raped by them. When her mother saw the bruises on her daughter's body, she called the police. Once again, however, the courts were lenient and Fred and Rose escaped with a fine.

Before too long, however, they killed again when another woman moved in to look after the children. Lynda Gough was murdered, dismembered and buried under the floor of the garage. Again, she was buried without her fingers and toes.

Their first son, Stephen, was born in August 1973 and a few months later they abducted 15 year-old Carol Ann Cooper. After sexually assaulting her for a time, she was strangled, dismembered and buried in the usual fashion.

BELOW: Interior view of the basement of 25 Cromwell Street.

Lucy Partington, a 21 year-old student, was abducted on 27 December, 1974. She was abused in the cellar for a week and then killed, dismembered and buried. Fred was building extensions to the cellar and the house, and the bodies were finding their way into these construction projects.

Another three young women, Theresa Siegentahaler, aged 21, Shirley Hubbard, aged 15, and Juanita Mott, aged 18, became victims of the Wests' sadistic practices between April 1974 and April 1975, their dismembered bodies being laid to rest under the floor of the cellar of 25 Cromwell Street.

Meanwhile, Anna Marie, Rena Costello's daughter was still being raped repeatedly. Fred even brought friends home to have sex with her.

An 18-year-old woman called Shirley Robinson, a former prostitute, became pregnant with Fred's child after having relationships with both of the Wests. At the time, Rose was pregnant with the child of one of her West Indian clients and while Fred tolerated this, Rose did not like the fact that he was having a child with another woman. In the summer of 1977, Shirley was murdered and, with her unborn child, was buried in the garden – the cellar was full.

Alison Chambers joined her in the garden in May 1977.

Anna Marie had by now moved out and Fred shifted his attentions to his other two daughters, Heather and Mae. Two more children followed – Barry in 1980 and Rosemary Junior, not Fred's child, in 1982. Yet another daughter, Lucyanna followed in 1983.

In 1986, daughter Heather made the mistake of telling a friend about what her father had been doing to her. Not long after, she was buried in the garden alongside the others. It is believed that they probably carried on their abductions, but 25 Cromwell Street was now full up and it is likely that bodies were disposed of elsewhere.

It was not until August 1992 that it all began to unravel. A girl that Fred had raped told a friend who went to the police. The pair were arrested, but, incredibly, the case against them collapsed when key witnesses withdrew their testimony. However, the police were now very interested in Fred and Rose and especially in Heather's disappearance.

On 24 February 1994, there was a knock at the door of 25 Cromwell Road. It was the police with a search warrant. Before too long, they were digging up bones in the garden. The next day, Fred West confessed, withdrew his confession and then confessed again.

Charged with 12 murders, Fred hanged himself with strips of bedsheet in his cell at Winson Green Prison, Birmingham, on New Year's Day, 1995.

Rose went to trial pleading innocence, but was found guilty on each of ten counts of murder. She is currently serving ten life sentences, with a minimum of 25 years, but says that she will never leave prison.

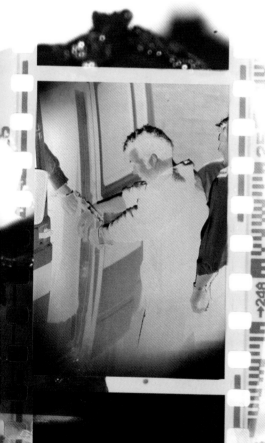

LEFT: Fred West is led away by guards after appearing at Gloucester Magistrates Court.

MENENDEZ
BROTHERS

722 ELM DRIVE,
BEVERLY HILLS, USA

IT WAS A WARM SUNDAY EVENING IN BEVERLY HILLS. JOSE AND KITTY MENENDEZ WERE ENJOYING A PEACEFUL NIGHT IN AT THEIR $4 MILLION (£2 MILLION), 23-ROOM MEDITERRANEAN STYLE MANSION IN ELM DRIVE. THE MAID HAD THE NIGHT OFF, AND THE COUPLE WERE DOZING IN FRONT OF THE TV, WHEN THEIR TWO SONS BROKE INTO THE HOUSE BRANDISHING SHOT GUNS. THE CARNAGE THAT FOLLOWED TURNED THIS LUXURIOUS FAMILY HOME INTO A NOTORIOUS HOUSE OF DEATH.

As Sunday 20 August 1989 drew to a close, the warmth of the day remained. At 722 Elm Drive, a 23-room mansion that had previously been rented by rock stars such as Elton John and Prince, all was quiet. The owners, 47 year-old wealthy record company executive, Jose Menendez, and his 44 year-old blond-haired, green-eyed wife, Kitty, relaxed in the family room at the back of the house, alternately dozing and watching Roger Moore go through the motions in a video of the James Bond film, *The Spy Who Loved Me*. Kitty looked younger than her years and Jose was fit and tanned from playing tennis.

It was 10pm, but the house's elaborate security system had not yet been switched on and the gates were open. The house was set back from the road in front of it, a thick curtain of trees and bushes surrounded by a high iron fence protecting its inhabitants from prying eyes.

A small car pulled into the drive and stopped in front of the house. Two men in their early 20's clambered out. While one man walked in the direction of the house, the other went round to the back of the car and took something from the boot. He then caught up on the other and the pair entered the house's study through a set of French doors. From the study, they made their way to the family room, hearing the film's dialogue as they approached. In the room, in which the only light was the light from the television screen, they saw Jose and Kitty.

Jose was asleep on the brown leather sofa, sitting at the end nearest to the door through which they had entered. His feet were resting on the coffee table drawn up to the sofa. Beside his feet, on the table, lay the remnants of a berry and ice cream dessert. Kitty was stretched out, lengthwise, on the sofa, a blanket covering her body, her head resting in her husband's lap. She, too, dozed.

The two men each carried a 12 gauge Mossberg shotgun. One of them slowly raised his gun and fired it twice at the sleeping Jose. One round shattered the glass of the room's French doors, the other hit him in the right arm. He barely moved before another bullet immobilized him completely. The man walked up behind him, put the barrel of the shotgun against the back of his head and blew off a chunk of his skull large enough to fit a man's fist in the gap it left.

Kitty woke up to the horror of feeling her husband's blood spurting on her. She leapt up and took a couple of steps before being shot in the right leg and right arm. Collapsing between the sofa and the coffee table, she managed to get up again. Desperately trying to stay on her feet, she tried to walk but another round brought her to the ground once more. As she lay there, the attackers ruthlessly pumped more bullets into her. She was hit in the thigh, breaking her leg, the right arm and the left breast, perforating a lung. She was still alive, however, and tried to crawl away.

The shooters had no more shotgun bullets, but they had to make sure Kitty was dead, as she would be able to recognize them if she lived. So, one of them ran back out to the car and brought back some birdshot. They re-loaded and one of them put his gun against her left cheek and pulled the trigger. A 25cm (1 in) hole was blasted through her cheek, fracturing her jaw and dislodging four of her teeth. They shot her four times in the head, altogether, three times in the face. Her left thumb was later found to have been almost severed, it seemed as if she had raised her hand to block out her view of the men trying to kill her.

Finally, one of the men shot each of their victims in the left knee, from the back, a characteristic sign of a Mafia shooting. But this was no Mafia shooting, and the two men were very well known to Jose and Kitty. They were, in fact, their two sons: 21-year-old Lyle Menendez and his eighteen-year-old brother Erik.

The boys had planned the murders meticulously. There would not be a problem with fingerprints as this was their home and their prints would be expected to be all over it. They drove to Mulholland Drive and threw the guns into a canyon

ABOVE: Defence attorney
Leslie Abramson
describes the crime
scene during the retrial
of brothers Lyle and
Erik Menendez for
the murders of their
parents, 22 November,
1995.

and then created their alibi by going to see a Batman film. Returning to 722 Elm Drive, Lyle phoned the police, in apparent distress, telling them, incoherently, that his parents had been shot.

At first, the police were sympathetic, and they had no reason to treat the boys as suspects. However, not long after the killings, Lyle and Erik began to spend their multi-million dollar inheritance lavishly. Just three days after the crime, for instance, they bought themselves $15,000 (£7,500) Rolex watches and it is estimated that they blew as much as $1 million (£500,000) in the ensuing six months.

Erik was the weaker of the two boys, and, one night it all became too much for him. He confessed all to his psychiatrist. When Lyle found out, he threatened the psychiatrist. However, he need not have worried for the moment as the rule of patient-therapist confidentiality applied and the psychiatrist was unable to inform the police. Eventually, however, he told the police what he knew and the brothers were indicted for the murder of their parents.

The trial became one of the most sensational in American criminal history, after the judge ruled that the public interest in the case was so great that a TV camera would be allowed into the court and the trial would be shown live on American TV. America watched, spellbound, as Leslie Abramson, Erik's defence attorney claimed that the brothers had been driven to kill their father after suffering abuse by him, including sexual abuse, throughout their lives. The brothers appeared arrogant and spoilt, smiling and waving to friends and family and smirking when they answered questions. It was as if they thought there was no way in the world they would not walk free.

After a lengthy trial, however, it seemed as if they might be right. The juries – there was one for each brother – both failed to reach a verdict and a second trial was called.

This time, there was no doubt. The tactics of the defence were unsuccessful and the Menendez brothers were found guilty of two counts of first-degree murder, plus conspiracy to commit murder.

On 2 July 1996, Lyle and Erik were sentenced to life in prison without possibility of parole. They were sent to separate prisons and have not seen or spoken to each other ever since.

JEFFREY DAHMER
213 OXFORD APARTMENTS,
MILWAUKEE, USA

WHEN POLICE ENTERED 213 OXFORD APARTMENTS ON 22 JULY 1991, THEY EXPECTED TO SETTLE A DOMESTIC DISPUTE BETWEEN TWO HOMOSEXUAL LOVERS AND LEAVE AS QUICKLY AND AS QUIETLY AS POSSIBLE. LITTLE DID THEY KNOW THAT THE HORRIFIC SCENES THEY WOULD ENCOUNTER IN JEFFREY DAHMER'S SMALL MILWAUKEE APARTMENT WOULD HAUNT THEM FOR THE REST OF THEIR LIVES.

On 22 July 1991, two police officers spied a short black man wearing what looked like handcuffs in the vicinity of Marquette University in Milwaukee. Their first thought was that he had escaped arrest and they immediately apprehended him. His name was Tracy Edwards and he began babbling about a 'weird dude' who had invited him up to his apartment, put the handcuffs on him and threatened him with a knife.

The officers thought it sounded like a lovers' tiff, but they decided to investigate and knocked on the door of apartment 213 in the Oxford Apartments at 924 North 25th Street. It was opened by a well-groomed, good-looking, 31-year-old man with blond hair.

He seemed very calm and rational and his apartment looked reasonably tidy, but a strange smell pervaded the place. When he went to get the key to the handcuffs from the bedroom, Edwards warned the officers that he had a knife in there, and one of the officers followed him. On his way, however, he noticed photographs lying around, depicting dismembered bodies and, bizarrely, skulls in a refrigerator. He shouted back to his colleague to cuff the blond man and arrest him. The blond man struggled as the other cop tried to put the cuffs on him, but was quickly subdued.

The first officer decided to look in the fridge. Opening the door, he froze in horror, the blood draining from his face. A pair of eyes stared out at him from a disembodied head. 'There's a f---ing head in the refrigerator!' he screamed.

The freezer contained another three heads, wrapped tidily in plastic bags. In a wardrobe in the bedroom he found a stockpot containing decomposed hands and a penis. On the shelf above were two skulls. There were male genitalia, preserved in formaldehyde. There were also photographs in a filing cabinet, taken as the victims died. In one, a man's head was shown, lying in the sink; another depicted a victim, cut neatly open from neck to groin; others showed victims, still alive, in erotic poses.

Jeffrey Dahmer, the blond man, was born in Milwaukee in 1960, but grew up in Akron, Ohio. To begin with he was an ordinary, happy little boy. As he grew older, however, he became tense and extremely shy. He would collect dead animals and strip the flesh from them.

In his late teenage years, he seemed completely unmotivated. Instead of thinking about girls and a future career, he was locked into a gruesome fantasy world of death and dismemberment. By now he was drinking a lot and was considered a loner and an alcoholic by classmates.

When Dahmer was almost eighteen his parents divorced, and it was around this time that he committed his first murder. He invited Steven Hicks, an eighteen-year-old hitchhiker back to his house, and hit him over the head with a barbell, because he 'didn't want him to leave'. He cut up Hicks's body and buried it in the woods behind his house.

LEFT: Tony Hughes, a victim of serial killer Jeffrey Dahmer.

OPPOSITE LEFT: A woman named Esther, a friend of Jeffrey Dahmer, explaining how they used to talk about the end of the world.

OPPOSITE RIGHT: Evidence tape and a lock seals the door to 213 Oxford Apartments.

EVIDENCE
DO NOT HANDLE

There's a
f****ing
head in the
refrigerator!

ABOVE: Milwaukee policemen carry away human remains belonging to the victims of serial killer Jeffrey Dahmer.

In January 1979, having dropped out of university, Jeffrey joined the army. As with university, however, his drinking made life impossible and, after a couple of years in Germany, he was given an early discharge. He moved in with his grandmother back in Milwaukee.

A string of offences followed – drunkenness, disorderly conduct and then indecent exposure and child molesting; he was reported to have masturbated in front of two boys. He persuaded the judge that he had, in fact, just been urinating, and was put on probation for a year.

Dahmer had, by this time, already killed his second victim, Steven Toumi, who he met in a gay bar and killed in a hotel room in September 1987. He stuffed his body into a large suitcase, took it to the basement of his grandmother's house, had sex with it and masturbated over it before dismembering it and disposing of it in the rubbish.

His third victim was fourteen-year-old Native American, Jamie Doxtator. The fourth was Richard Guerro, in March 1988.

He moved into his own apartment in September 1988 and the next day he picked up a thirteen-year-old Laotian boy, Saravane Sinthasomphone, who agreed to pose for photographs for $50.00 (£25.00). By grim coincidence, he was the older brother of a boy Dahmer would kill in 1991.

He did not kill Saravane but, when the boy returned home, his parents realized he had been drugged, and Dahmer was arrested for sexual assault. He pleaded guilty, claiming he had thought the boy was older. Even as he awaited sentencing however, he struck again, killing Anthony Sears, a handsome black model. Dahmer boiled his skull to remove the skin and painted it grey.

In court, he put on the kind of manipulative performance only a psychopath can, and he got away with five years' probation. He was also ordered to spend a year in the House of Correction under 'work release', which meant he went to work during the day and returned to jail at night. He was released after just ten months and went to live with his grandmother, before moving into his rooms in the Oxford apartments in May 1990.

Exactly a year later, a naked fourteen-year-old Laotian, Konerak Sinthasomphone, was found wandering in Dahmer's neighbourhood. The boy was incoherent, having already been drugged by Dahmer. When the police arrived, they took the boy back to the flat where Dahmer calmly told them that Konerak was his nineteen-year-old boyfriend and that they had had a drunken argument. The police handed the boy over to Dahmer, noting a strange smell in the apartment. A few hours later, Konerak was dead.

From September 1987 to July 1991, Jeffrey Dahmer killed 16 men, ranging in age from 14 to 31. He would pick up his victim at a gay bar, lure him back to his grandmother's basement or his flat to pose for photographs and then would offer him a drugged drink, strangle him, masturbate on the body or even have sex with it. He would then cut the corpse up and dispose of it. He took photographs throughout and sometimes boiled the skull, to remove the flesh, keeping it and other body parts as mementos. He began experimenting with various chemical methods to dispose of the flesh and bones. The residue would be poured down a drain or flushed down the toilet. He often preserved the genitals in formaldehyde.

He also ate some of the flesh of his victims, claiming that, by doing so, they would come alive in him again. He experimented with seasoning and meat tenderizers.

Before they died, he sometimes tried to perform a kind of lobotomy on his victims. After drugging them, he would drill a hole in their skulls and inject muriatic acid into their brains. He was trying to create a functioning zombie-like creature that he could exercise ultimate control over. Needless to say, most died during this procedure.

Although, at his trial, his counsel tried to prove he was insane, he was found guilty, receiving 15 life sentences, a total of 957 years in prison.

On the morning of 28 November 1994, at Columbia Correctional Institute in Wisconsin, another inmate smashed Dahmer's skull with a blunt instrument (accounts differ as to what weapon was actually used). He died in an ambulance on the way to hospital.

BELOW: A sketch by Jeffrey L Dahmer, showing a temple he intended to build using the body parts of his victims, 4 February, 1992.

DAVID
KORESH

Mount Carmel,
Waco, Texas, USA

THE ENTRANCE TO THE NOTORIOUS
MOUNT CARMEL RANCH IS NOW
PROTECTED BY A HOME-MADE BARRIER,
AND HANDWRITTEN SIGNS INDICATE
THAT ENTRY IS AT THE VISITORS OWN
RISK DUE TO BROKEN GLASS AND OTHER
POTENTIAL HAZARDS LITTERING THE SITE.
THE MEDIA AND GOVERNMENT AGENTS
MAY HAVE LEFT THE AREA, BUT SCARS
LEFT BY THE WACO ASSAULT, SIEGE AND
SUBSEQUENT FIRE, CAN STILL BE SEEN ON
THE LANDSCAPE.

David Koresh was born Vernon David Howell in 1959, in Houston, Texas, to a 14 year-old single mother and a father who did not hang around for long. An abusive stepfather helped to complete the picture and round off the manipulative psychopath who would become David Koresh, messianic leader of the Branch Davidian cult, and a radical spin-off from the Seventh Day Adventists. At school, the children called him 'Mister Retardo' because of his learning difficulties, but, nonetheless, by the age of 12, he had learned the New Testament by heart.

Howell joined the Branch Davidians in the early 1980s, after moving to its headquarters at a ranch renamed the Mount Carmel Centre, near Waco. Handsome but aggressive, he soon harboured ambitions to be its leader. To this end, he entered into a sexual relationship with sect leader, Lois Roden, then in her late 50s. By 1983, he was claiming to have the gift of prophecy.

A power struggle with Lois Roden's son, George, ensued, which Roden won, temporarily, evicting Howell and some followers from Mount Carmel. Around this time, Howell made a pilgrimage to Israel, claiming that while there he had a vision that he was the modern-day Cyrus (messiah). He also proclaimed to his followers that he was the 'Son of God'. Further to this, he proclaimed that he would, from that point on, be permitted to indulge in polygamy. He began to sleep with many of the women in his group, even girls as young as 12 years of age.

In an effort to prove his status, George Roden challenged Howell to a contest to see which of them could raise the dead, digging up a corpse to do so. As their disputes escalated, Howell and some followers attacked Mount Carmel, and disaster was only avoided with the intervention of the police, who found Howell and his men firing at Roden. They were acquitted of attempted murder.

In 1988, however, Roden was convicted of the murder of a man who argued with him that Howell was the Messiah and

Howell took over Mount Carmel, assuming leadership of the Branch Davidians.

In 1990, Howell began styling himself 'David Koresh' because he wanted to establish a link as the true heir to King David and 'Koresh' meant 'death' or 'Cyrus' – meaning messiah. He provided strict guidelines as to how cult members were to live their days, making amendments to the rules as and when he pleased and delivering long, rambling sermons relentlessly, night or day. The rules, of course, did not apply to him. He was permitted food that they were not, he could sleep until noon if he so desired, and he was allowed to drink alcohol, strictly forbidden to Branch Davidians.

Koresh continued to select whichever female took his fancy and fathered numerous children with the women in the Mount Carmel compound. One woman later testified that she was sexually molested by Koresh at the age of ten and Koresh then read her passages from the Bible. He gave long, rambling sermons that explained sexual matters and practices and girls were groomed to believe that marriage and relationships with him were a natural thing and, in fact, desirable. One girl, eventually released during the later siege, was reportedly distraught on realizing she would never be one of Koresh's wives.

It was later learned that Koresh taught the children in the compound to call their natural parents 'dogs', while he was 'father'. Meanwhile, children, not Koresh's were called 'bastards'. He ensured that normal familial relationships were eradicated and all were taught to depend on him and God. It was not long before he was proclaiming that he was God.

The children were also taught about weapons and gun-use, and were severely disciplined for the most trivial breach of the rules with isolation, food deprivation and serious beatings. There was a 'whipping room' in the basement where children could be beaten out of earshot of the adults in the compound.

By 1992, martyrdom had entered the Davidian lexicon, and Koresh was actively engaged in preparing his followers for martyrdom for the Branch Davidian cause. He was also stockpiling food and an arsenal of weapons and ammunition for use against the enemy, the defectors, dissidents and, above all, government agents that he described as the 'Babylonians'.

By 1993, however, the Bureau of Alcohol, Tobacco and firearms had been alerted to the activities of the Branch Davidians. They had been selling guns and ammunition and, although what they were engaging in was not illegal, they were also said to be selling rapid-fire automatic weapons – which was. When a parcel being delivered to them fell apart, the delivery man found grenade casings inside and reported them to the authorities.

On 28 February 1993, more than 70 BATF agents moved in. They had been watching Mount Carmel for some time and had even infiltrated the compound with some undercover operatives. The raid was a disaster. As a Blackhawk helicopter from the local national guard hovered above, gunfire broke out, in which four BATF agents and five Branch Davidians were killed. Koresh and 16 more agents were wounded.

It would be the beginning of an intense 51-day stand-off that was followed daily by television viewers around the world. The FBI were brought in to manage things and they began to broadcast loud noise at the inhabitants of the compound – Tibetan Buddhist chants, bagpipes, seagulls crying, helicopters, dentist drills, sirens, dying rabbits, a train, and songs by Alice Cooper and Nancy Sinatra. Koresh would respond to attempts at negotiation with a reading from the Bible and the stalemate would continue. Nonetheless, he began to release children.

Koresh repeatedly won time by claiming that he wanted to observe Passover or that he wanted to complete his writing of a manuscript about the meaning of the Seven Seals. Eventually, however, as April passed, new secretary of state, Janet Reno, gave her approval for a raid to bring the siege to a close. They would use CS gas, deployed by a couple of combat engineering vehicles to force the cult members to leave the compound. Shortly before dawn, on Monday, 19 April, they moved in.

The Branch Davidians immediately opened fire, but were unable to make an impression on the vehicles that punched holes in the walls and pumped in the gas. As this work continued, shortly before noon, flames could be seen inside the buildings. They spread fast and were accompanied by several loud explosions and gunfire.

It was feared that the Branch Davidians had decided on a mass suicide – which it was, more or less. Only nine emerged alive. When investigators moved in, they found 80 bodies, 23 of them children under 17 – 14 were later discovered to have been fathered by Koresh.

Rumours that Koresh had escaped through an underground tunnel complex proved to be false, when his body was later identified from dental records. He had been shot in the head.

BELOW: The Branch Davidian compound explodes in a burst of flames 19 April, 1993, ending the standoff between cult leader David Koresh and his followers and the FBI near Waco, Texas.

THE TENT JAIL

TENT CITY JAIL, PHOENIX, ARIZONA, USA

TENT CITY JAIL, IN PHOENIX, ARIZONA, IS ONE OF THE MOST BRUTAL PRISONS IN THE US, AND ITS SHERIFF IS ONE OF THE NATION'S TOUGHEST LAWMEN. IN THE EYES OF JOE ARPAIO, PRISON IS ALL ABOUT PUNISHMENT, AND HE MAKES SURE THAT PUNISHMENT IS EXACTLY WHAT HIS INMATES GET.

Joe Arpaio is known as 'America's toughest sheriff'. Denounced by civil liberties organizations, he claims to have the ambition of making Maricopa County Jail in Phoenix the most populated jail in the US. He can certainly lay claim to making it one of the most brutal. His prison philosophy holds that prisoners should be treated as harshly as is legally possible. For him, prison is not about rehabilitation; it is simply about punishment.

In 1993, the jails in the county were filled to overflowing and Arpaio was reluctant to free prisoners to ease conditions. So, he obtained a number of surplus military tents and erected them outside the jail. The project was inexpensive – all he needed was cement for bases for the tents, some secure fencing and electricity to run the heating, cooling and security lights. He was saving the taxpayer a fortune; a new jail would have cost around $70 million (£35 million). His tents Jail now has a capacity of 2,000 inmates.

Arpaio has made savings in other ways. Coffee was taken off the prison menu, saving $150,000 (£75,000) a year. Serving surplus, outdated, green bologna sandwiches saved on food bills by another $500,000 (£250,000). The removal of salt

and pepper from dining hall tables saved the taxpayer $20,000 (£10,000) a year. Food costs for inmates are now 30 cents (15 pence) a day; the prison's guard dogs get food worth $1.10 (55 pence) a day.

Smoking is forbidden, pornographic magazines, a staple of any prison, are banned and inmates are not allowed weightlifting equipment. Only G-rated (family-viewing) films are available to watch and the cable TV system only shows educational material such as Animal Planet, the Disney Channel and the Weather Channel.

Arpaio has also reintroduced chain gangs for both men and women prisoners. Inmates work eight hours a day, six days a week, building fire breaks, clearing up rubbish and burying people in the county cemetery. Their free labour puts thousands of dollars back into the state economy. The chain gang is not the only retro feature Arpaio has introduced. Inmates wear the striped clothing that convicts used to wear and, bizarrely, pink underwear. He had noticed that the normal white underwear, which was labelled with Maricopa County Sheriff's Office, was being smuggled out of the prison and sold. So, he had it all dyed pink, believing men would never

BELOW: Inmates walk through the courtyard at Joe Arpaio's tent jail in Phoenix on 31 January 2008.

ABOVE: A group of women chain gang members celebrate the 5th anniversary of Joe Arpaio's 'Tent City', with cake and punch, before heading back to their duties, 3 August 1998.

wear underwear of that colour. To his consternation, however, orders for it came flooding in, but he decided to take advantage by turning it into a commercial operation, raising funds for the work of his office. He has since introduced pink handcuffs, and, realizing the calming effect pink has on violent inmates, has had sheets, socks, towels and other items dyed pink.

One of the worst things about the prison, however, is the stifling Arizona heat. Temperatures can reach a 38°C (100°F). Arpaio, of course, has no sympathy. 'It's 120°F in Iraq and the soldiers are living in tents and they didn't commit any crimes, so shut your mouths,' he says in his characteristically unsympathetic way. Still, he is not all bad – he allows them to strip down to their pink underwear when it gets too hot.

There have been a number of high-profile cases highlighting the more extreme side of sheriff Arpaio's regime. Scott Norberg died in custody after being shot a number of times with a stun-gun. The medical examiner found he had died of 'positional asphyxia', but Arpaio and his men were cleared of blame. Norberg's parents sued and settled for $8.25 million (£4.125

million) after it was found the sheriff's office had destroyed important evidence.

Brian Crenshaw was beaten into a coma by Arpaio's guards. After he died in the local hospital, Arpaio said, 'the man fell off a bunk.'

Richard Post, a paraplegic inmate, was pushed so hard into a restraint chair by guards that his neck was broken. The incident was captured on video and the guards laugh and joke on film as Post is injured.

The Irish government refused to extradite Patrick Colleany, a Roman Catholic priest accused of molesting an alter boy in Scottsdale, Arizona in 1978. Stating that, 'it was the duty of any Irish court to see that no citizen was handed over to such a regime'. They described Arpaio as a man who 'appeared to take a chillingly sadistic pleasure in his role as incarcerator' and before gloated over the inhumane treatment he dishes out to his inmates.'

In May 2007, Arpaio asked the Los Angeles authorities to transfer Paris Hilton, incarcerated for driving offences, to Maricopa to serve her sentence. His request was 'respectfully declined'.

THOMAS HAMILTON
DUNBLANE PRIMARY SCHOOL, DUNBLANE, SCOTLAND

THE MASSACRE COMMITTED BY THOMAS HAMILTON AT DUNBLANE PRIMARY SCHOOL ON 13 MARCH 1996, SHOCKED AND HORRIFIED THE BRITISH PUBLIC. HOW COULD SOMEBODY WALK, UNCHALLENGED, INTO A SCHOOL, CARRYING NO LESS THAN FOUR GUNS, AND BEGIN FIRING INDISCRIMINATELY AT INNOCENT CHILDREN AND TEACHERS INSIDE? THE SCALE OF THE TRAGEDY BEGGARED BELIEF, AS DID THE FEELINGS OF ANGER, GRIEF AND LOSS SHARED BY US ALL.

Thomas Watt Hamilton had been experiencing some problems. There had been complaints to the police about the youth clubs he ran and his suspect behaviour towards some of the young boys who attended them. He had been known to take photographs of boys, semi-naked, without the consent of their parents. He blamed the rumours about him for the failure, in 1993, of the shop he had owned and had struggled against what he described as persecution by the police and the Boy Scout movement as, in recent months, he had attempted to set up another boys' club. He complained to his local MP and even wrote to the Queen.

Around 8.15am on 13 March 1996, Hamilton stopped scraping the ice off the windscreen of his white van outside his house in Kent Road, Stirling, to have a conversation with a passing neighbour. The neighbour reported later that there was nothing untoward about the conversation, just the customary grumbles about the icy weather.

A little later, he got in the van and drove off in the direction of the town of Dunblane, about 10km (6 miles) to the north of Stirling. He arrived at his destination, Dunblane Primary School in Doune Road, at around 9.30am, parking beside a telegraph pole in one of the school's car parks. Climbing out of the van, he took a pair of pliers and cut the telephone wires at the foot of the pole. These did not connect the school to the telephone network, however. They were, instead, linked to nearby houses.

Hamilton set off across the car park, carrying two 9mm Browning HP pistols and two Smith & Wesson .357 Magnum revolvers. He had 743 cartridges and was about to use 109 of them. Entering the school through a door on its west side, to avoid being seen, he made his way towards the gym.

Dunblane was a large school, with 640 pupils, and this made morning assemblies for the entire school impossible. Therefore, they were held in rotation, one each morning for a different year group. So, on

this day, all primary one, two and three classes, the youngest classes in the school, had attended assembly from 9.10am until 9.30am.

Primary 1/13 was due to have a PE session after assembly and had, consequently, changed in readiness prior to going into the assembly hall. It was a class of 28 children, taught by 47-year-old Gwen Mayor. 25 of the children were five years old and the remaining three were six years old. A PE teacher, Eileen Harrild, was already in the gym with supervisory assistant, Mary Blake, when the class arrived and while the adults had a discussion about the lesson, the children were asked to wait in the centre of the hall.

As they were talking, Eileen Harrild heard a noise behind her and turned round to see what it was. What she was hearing were probably the random shots Thomas Hamilton was firing into the stage in the assembly hall and the girls' toilet, which was located just outside the gym. As she watched the door, he entered the gym. He was dressed in a dark jacket, black corduroy trousers and a woollen hat. He was wearing ear protectors and in his hand, to her horror, she saw a gun.

A couple of steps into the gym, Hamilton opened fire, shooting indiscriminately. Eileen Harrild was immediately hit in both arms, her right hand and left breast. She staggered into a storage area abutting the gym and a number of terrified children scrambled in after her. Gwen Mayor was shot and fell to the floor, dead. Mary Blake was also hit but made it to the storage area, ushering a group of the children in front of her. In the store, shocked and frightened children cowered, blood pooling on the floor from their wounds. Meanwhile, in the gym, the other children screamed and sobbed.

Hamilton fired 29 shots, killing one child and wounding a number of others. He walked up one side of the gym, firing at them. He then moved into the centre and, walking in a semi-circle, fired 16 bullets into a group of pupils who lay on the floor, trying to hide or already wounded.

Callously, he approached them and began to fire at them from point-blank range. A pupil from another class, who was running an errand for his teacher, heard the commotion and looked into the gym. Spotting him, Hamilton opened fire. But the boy ran off, fortunately injured only by some broken glass.

Hamilton walked to the southern end of the gym and fired another 24 bullets. He fired through a window, probably at an adult who was walking past outside and then opened the fire-escape door and let loose another four shots.

Stepping through the door, he fired at the library cloakroom, wounding teacher Grace Tweddle in the head. He then turned his attention to a temporary classroom, firing nine shots into it. The teacher had already heard noises and had instructed her class to get onto the floor, a decision which saved their lives as bullets rammed into seats and desks.

Hamilton returned to the gym and opened fire again. Then he suddenly drew a revolver from his pocket, placed the barrel in his mouth and pulled the trigger. He fell to the ground, dying.

Fifteen children and their teacher, Gwen Mayor, lay dead around him. One other pupil would die later in hospital. The whole tragic episode had taken just four minutes.

BELOW: Photograph taken by Dunblane schoolteacher, Gwen Mayor, of the children in her 29-strong Primary One class. This picture was taken weeks before Thomas Hamilton entered the school gym and killed Mayor and 16 of her pupils.

GIANNI VERSACE
OCEAN DRIVE,
MIAMI BEACH, FLORIDA, USA

THE VERSACE MANSION ON OCEAN DRIVE HAS BECOME THE MOST PHOTOGRAPHED BUILDING IN FLORIDA. THESE DAYS THE SPANISH STYLE VILLA IS AN ULTRA-FASHIONABLE BOUTIQUE HOTEL, AND IN ITS HEYDAY THE HOUSE WAS REGULARLY FREQUENTED BY CELEBRITY GUESTS SUCH AS MADONNA, JACK NICHOLSON AND ELTON JOHN. IT WAS HERE, ON 15 JULY 1997, THAT THE INTERNATIONALLY RENOWNED FASHION DESIGNER, GIANNI VERSACE, WAS MURDERED BY THE RAMPANT 'GAY PSYCHO SERIAL KILLER' ANDREW CUNANAN.

When Gianni Versace arrived in Miami Beach on 12 July 1997, the fifty-year-old fashion guru was exhausted. He had recently completed a European tour and wanted to rest for a while. But business had never been better. Profits from his companies were rolling in at around $900 million (£450 million) a year and his clothes were loved by film stars and royalty alike. So, now, as he always did when he came to Miami, he would relax in his favourite spots, gay bars like The Twist, the KGB Club or Liquid. In the mornings he would venture out, having divested himself of his host of retainers and bodyguards, and walk alone from his exuberantly fronted mansion on 11 Street to the News Café on Ocean Drive, where he would enjoy a coffee and slip out of his frenetic world for a while.

What Versace failed to notice was the presence of a shadow on many of these walks.

Andrew Cunanan had been looking for Versace in all the usual clubs and bars, and finally, he had caught up with him. It was not the first time he had seen him. A few years earlier, both had attended the same party. Versace, on arriving, cast his eye around the room, lighting on the handsome face of Cunanan. He was there with Eli Gould, one of the wealthy,

BELOW: Mug shot of Andrew Cunanan.

older men who befriended and bedded the good-looking young man. Gould had introduced Cunanan to the world of movie stars and people of influence, and Cunanan loved it. Now, Gianni Versace was making a beeline for him and even seemed to recognize him. Actually, Versace was mistaken, but when he asked the young man where they had met, suggesting 'Lago di Como?' Cunanan coyly played along and said how nice it was of him to remember.

Now, on the morning of 15 July 1997, he was once again close to the great man. As Versace pulled out the key to his ornate gate, Cunanan got closer still. He stepped up behind the fashion designer, put a pistol to his head and, hardly batting an eyelid, pumped two .40-calibre bullets into it.

It was not the first murder Cunanan had committed, but it would mark the end of a bloody road for him. The media frenzy was extraordinary. The police, who until now had been slapdash in their approach to this unfathomable spree killer who seemed to vanish every time he killed, taunting them with photos and calling cards, began to work harder at catching him.

Cunanan had a brilliant mind, spoke seven languages and possessed a chameleon-like capacity to become different people. It had served him well in the world of gay bars and pick-up joints he frequented, working as a male prostitute. And, with his male model looks, he had been good at it. Wealthy businessmen, married men with families, kept him as their guilty secret, plying him with credit cards, cars and apartments, in return for his services.

Beneath it all, however, there was an irrational anger, ready to erupt at any time, especially as he reached his late 20s and his looks began to fade. At 28, he had put on weight and let his hair grow. He was drinking vodka and taking the pain killers he had previously sold to earn some extra cash. In San Francisco he began to descend into the depraved world of gay porn. Orgies, leather and chains became his currency, and he appeared in several porn films.

Deserted by his wealthy providers and eaten up by jealousy over two of his lovers who had begun an affair, he also began to kill.

In April 1997, Cunanan came to suspect two of his friends, David Madson and Jeff Trail of having an affair, and he became irrationally jealous. He flew to Minneapolis, where they lived, and at a meeting of the three men where Trail and Madson hoped to reassure Cunanan that nothing was going on, Cunanan became furious and killed Trail with a claw hammer.

Madson fled with him in a red Jeep Cherokee, but Cunanan had left his backpack at Madson's apartment and inside were items identifying him. Approximately 72km (45 miles) north of Minneapolis, he pulled the vehicle over to the side of the road and pumped three bullets into Madson, killing him.

Cunanan was on a spree now and enjoying the release and the rush it gave him.

His next victim was probably randomly chosen. Lee Miglin had made his money from real-estate developments, and his company managed more than 10 million square metres (32 million square feet) of buildings throughout the midwest. His wife, Marilyn, who sold cosmetics and perfumes on the Home Shopping Network, was out of town on the evening of Saturday 3 May. At some point in the evening, Andrew Cunanan turned up and forced Miglin into his garage, where he tied his wrists and wrapped his face with duct tape, leaving only a hole through which he could breathe. He then began to torture him, reprising scenes from his favourite 'snuff film', Target for Torture. Finally, he stabbed him in the chest with a pair of pruning shears and slowly slit his throat with a hacksaw. In a final act of fury, he placed the body under the dead man's car, a 1994 Lexus, and drove back and forward over it.

Cunanan spent that night in the house, watching some videos and sleeping in Lee and Marilyn's bed. Next morning, he set off in the Lexus. When David Madson's Jeep was discovered, a few blocks away, the front seat was strewn with photographs of Cunanan. He was taunting the police and

ABOVE: The murder scene where world-famous fashion designer Gianni Versace was gunned down by crazed-killer Andrew Cunanan.

by the end of that day, he had made the FBI's list of America's top ten most wanted. His next victim was 45-year-old William Reese. Cunanan wanted his 1995 Chevrolet pickup, and shot him at point-blank range in his kitchen.

The nation was horrified and the police were stumped by these seemingly motiveless killings. Theories were postulated as to what was driving Cunanan. Many in the gay community believed that he had discovered that he was HIV-positive and had gone out of his mind.

Cunanan, however, was on his way to Miami Beach to commit one more murder, this time premeditated – Gianni Versace.

After the killing of Versace, Miami Beach was getting too hot. Eventually, the authorities caught up with Cunanan, hiding out in a houseboat. As hundreds of police waited on the quayside and on neighbouring rooftops, a team boarded the vessel and moved from room to room looking for him. Eventually they found him, spreadeagled on the floor with a bullet hole just above the right ear on that once handsome head. Now no one would ever know why he did what he did.

HEAVEN'S GATE

18241 COLINA NORTA,
SAN DIEGO, USA

18241 COLINA NORTE IS A BEAUTIFUL MEDITTERANEAN STYLE MANSION IN AN EXCLUSIVE AREA OF SAN DIEGO. IRONICALLY, FOR OVER 30 MEMBERS OF THE HEAVEN'S GATE CULT, THIS SANTA FE CUL-DE-SAC CAME TO REPRESENT A LITERAL DEAD-END, WHEN THE FLYING SAUCER THEY EXPECTED TO TRANSPORT THEM TO HEAVEN, FAILED TO MATERIALIZE.

HEAVEN'S GATE

The stench of decay was overpowering as deputy sheriff Robert Bunk approached the mansion at 18241 Colina Norte, in the quiet commuter town of Rancho Santa Fe in San Diego County, California. Nothing much happened in Rancho Santa Fe normally. The highest income community in the US, the area is mostly residential, with just one shopping avenue and a preponderance of large, expensive houses. As he stood in front of the door, deputy sheriff Bunk realized the stories were true: there were bodies in the house. He thought of Jonestown and called for back-up.

He and another officer were the first to enter the building. They found bodies lying everywhere, on beds or on bunks. At first, the corpses' short hair suggested that they were all male, and that is what they initially reported back to headquarters. There were 39 bodies, altogether, and further inspection revealed that 21 of them were in fact women. They were all white and their ages ranged from 26 to 72. Each of the deceased was dressed alike, in identical black shirts and tracksuit bottoms. On their feet, they wore brand-new black-and-white Nike trainers, possibly because of the Nike motto, 'Just do it'. Armband patches on their shirts read, 'Heaven's Gate Away Team'. This was almost certainly a reference to Star Trek: The Next Generation, in which a team of a few members, called the 'away team', went off on planetary explorations. A square purple cloth covered each face and upper body and each of them had three quarters and a five-dollar note in his or her pocket. Whenever they had left the house, it was later learned, they always carried exactly this amount of money so they had enough to get a taxi home or to make a phone call.

An eerie silence gripped the house as the officers went about their duty. On computer screens, images of alien-human hybrids flashed. Videos were discovered containing footage of the people in the mansion calmly making their farewells to family and friends. It was evident from these that there had been no coercion; these people had died willingly.

The San Diego County medical examiner

made a further shocking discovery. Seven members of the cult had been castrated, including their leader, Marshall Applewhite. Marshall Herff Applewhite was a leader of men from the outset. He lost his wife and two children as well as his job at the University of Alabama School of Music over an affair with a male student. In 1972, in his early 40s, he admitted himself to a psychiatric hospital.

Bonnie Lu Trousdale Nettles was four years older than him and a nurse at the hospital. She was a member of the Theosophical Society, an organization formed in 1875, by, among others, Madame Blavatsky, to advance the spiritual principles and search for 'Truth'. She encouraged Applewhite to join her in her work and in her life.

The two of them had a lot in common. They shared an interest in UFOs, astrology and science fiction, and started to believe that they were, in fact, earthly incarnations of alien beings with the mission on earth of saving as many people as possible in the coming end of the world. Bonnie left her four children and the two set out to spread the word and gather followers.

The message they preached said that their enemies would kill them and their followers and that their bodies would lie on the streets for 3.5 days before they would rise from the dead and ascend in a cloud to a higher level where they would exist with God. Their 'cloud' would arrive in the form of a spaceship.

After Applewhite had spent a humiliating four months in prison for credit card fraud, in 1975, the pair headed for the most fertile territory for finding people who would believe what they said – California. There, they started a group called Human Individual Metamorphosis and 25 people signed up. Following a meeting in the Oregon town of Waldport, to which 200 people turned up, another 20 joined them, abandoning their previous lives. One couple even left their 10 year-old daughter behind.

That same year, Applewhite and Nettles provided an exact date for the arrival of the spaceship. Their followers gathered together and waited on the given night. Nothing happened, of course, and Applewhite at least had the decency to apologize and invite anyone to leave who wanted to. But, for many, there was

BELOW: Members of the San Diego Medical Examiner's office carry the body of one Heaven's Gate cult member out of their head quarters at 18241 Colina Norte.

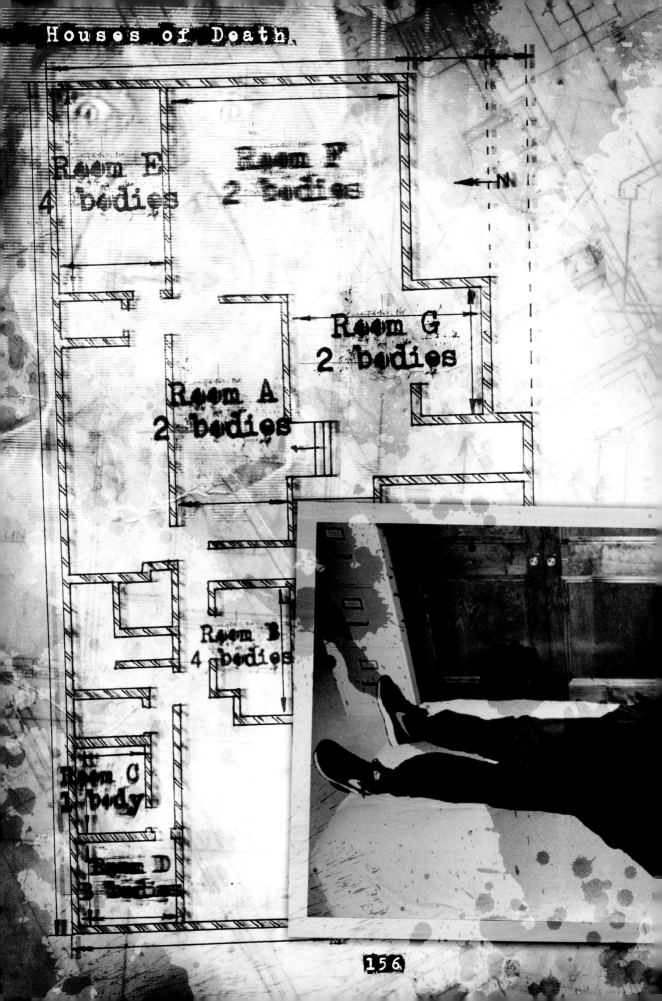

Room E
4 bodies

Room F
2 bodies

N

Room G
2 bodies

Room A
2 bodies

Room B
4 bodies

Room C
1 body

Room D
3 bodies

nowhere else to go and they had come this far in search of the 'next level'. They were not about to give up now.

The two leaders now asked everyone to cut their hair in the same, short style and to wear unisex clothes. They were encouraged to stick rigidly to their training regimen, to aspire to be genderless, eternal beings. Sexual contact was forbidden and privacy was not allowed. They became isolated from the rest of society, perceiving the media to be distorting what they stood for, and Applewhite encouraged 'crew-mindedness' – working and thinking together in preparation for the way they would have to be on the spaceship. They were all related, Applewhite claimed, with him as their father and Nettles as their grandmother. He called himself 'Do' and she became 'Ti'. Nonetheless, their numbers had fallen by the end of 1976, from 200 to only 80. As finances became difficult, they sold 'spaceship rides' for $433 (£216.00), and a legacy of $300,000 (£150,000) helped them out.

Ti/Nettles died of cancer in 1985 and, contrary to their teachings, did not resurrect. Applewhite said she had merely gone on ahead to make things ready for them and would, in fact, be piloting the mother ship when it arrived.

Having changed their name to Total Overcomers Anonymous, in 1993, they placed an advert in USA Today claiming that the end was near. Applewhite led his group to Rancho Santa Fe three years later in order to make preparations. They formed a web page design business called Higher Source and promoted their beliefs on the Internet. By now they were calling themselves Heaven's Gate.

A comet called Hale-Bopp was due to reach its brightest in our skies towards the end of March, 1997. Do informed his people that Ti had told him, telepathically, that Hale-Bopp was the sign they had been waiting for. An object in the wake of the comet was clearly the spaceship they had been expecting, he said. They bought a powerful, state-of-the-art telescope to have a closer look, but returned it to the shop, telling the bemused manager that it was no use as they had been unable to see their spaceship with it.

On Friday 21 March 1997, all 39 members went to a restaurant and ordered the exact same meal – salad and pot pies, followed by cheesecake. It would be their last meal on earth, because the next day the comet would be at its closest point.

On the Saturday, they dressed in their identical clothing and each filled an overnight bag with clothes, lip balm and a notebook. They split into three teams. The first group of 15 ate pudding or applesauce laced with barbiturate Phenobarbital, washing it down with vodka. They then lay on their beds or bunks and put plastic bags over their heads. The remainder tidied up after them, covering them with the purple shrouds. The next day, another 15 went through the same process. On Monday, seven more members followed and then, the final two.

Former members received videos of what had happened and the police were alerted.

There were no reported sightings of a spaceship in the area.

FAR LEFT: Floor plan of 18241 Colina Norte.

CENTRE: A photograph showing a participant in the "Heaven's Gate" mass suicide, provided by the San Diego County Sheriff's department, March 1997 file photo.

LUKE WOODHAM
PEARL HIGH SCHOOL,
MISSISSIPPI, USA

LUKE WOODHAM WAS ONE OF THOSE KIDS FOR WHOM HIGH SCHOOL WAS HELL. HE WAS A SOCIAL PARIAH - A NERD - WHO WAS EASILY SEDUCED BY SATANIST FRIENDS INTO BELIEVING HE COULD SUMMON DEMONS TO RIGHT THE WRONGS IN HIS LIFE. WOODHAM SET OUT ON 1 OCTOBER 1997 TO SETTLE A SCORE WITH AN EX GIRLFRIEND. IN HIS EYES, HE'D BEEN PUSHED TO THE BRINK, AND NOW HE WAS GOING TO PUSH BACK.

'Oh, Mr Myrick! I'm the one that gave you the discount on the pizza the other night.' 16-year-old, bespectacled Luke Woodham was speaking to the man who had just subdued him after his killing spree at Pearl High School in Mississippi, on 1 October 1997. Shocked assistant principal Joel Myrick, replied, 'What? Why did you do this to my kids?' Woodham replied, 'Mr Myrick, I've been wronged. The world has wronged me and I just couldn't take it anymore.'

Shortly before launching his spree, Woodham, often teased and called a 'nerd' by fellow students, had passed a chilling message to his friend and co-conspirator,

ABOVE: Woodham family photo.

Justin Sledge, trying to explain his actions. 'I am not insane, I am angry. I killed because people like me are mistreated every day. I did this to show society, push us and we will push back. All throughout my life, I was ridiculed, always beaten, always hated. Can you, society, truly blame me for what I do? Yes, you will. It was not a cry for attention, it was not a cry for help. It was a scream in sheer agony saying that if you can't pry your eyes open, if I can't do it through pacifism, if I can't show you through the displaying of intelligence, then I will do it

with a bullet.' The page ended with a line from the writings of German philosopher, Nietzsche, asking, 'How shall we comfort ourselves, the murderers of all murderers?'

Woodham was an angry young man. His girlfriend, Christina Menefee, had dumped him the previous year and it had devastated him. 'I didn't eat. I didn't sleep. I didn't want to live,' he sobbed later, in court. 'It destroyed me.' He had always been a loner in school and his home life was poor after the break-up of his parents' marriage. Therefore, his relationship with Christina had assumed an overwhelming importance to him. It was the first acceptance this school outcast had ever found.

Not long after the end of his relationship, he had become friendly with 18 year-old Grant Boyette, and 16-year-old Justin Sledge. Boyette and Sledge wore black and described themselves as Satanists. Boyette, who was fascinated with Adolf Hitler, was the leader of a group known as the Kroth, and they invited Woodham to join the Kroth, telling him that he had 'the potential to do something great'. Woodham felt at home with Boyette and his fellow Satanists. He also felt powerful. He claims that he and Boyette cast a spell on a teenager they did not like and he was killed in a traffic accident the following day. 'One second I was some kind of heart-broken idiot and the next second I had power over many things,' Woodham said later. 'My mind didn't know how to take it. You can send demons to go and do things,' he went on. 'I've seen them. I know what I was dealing with. I felt like I had complete control, complete power over things. I know it's real in spite of what people think.'

Boyette and Sledge brainwashed Woodham, telling him that murder was a viable means of achieving his aims. They repeatedly told him that if he shot Christina Menefee, he would never have to see her again and his problems would be over. Together, the group planned a raid on Pearl High School, with Woodham going in first as an assassin. They plotted to kill parents and massacre the school population.

As a dress rehearsal for the killings,

Woodham killed his pet dog, Sparkle. In his writings is a description of how he and an accomplice set fire to the dog and threw it into a pond. 'I'll never forget the sound of her breaking under my might,' he wrote. 'I hit her so hard I knocked the fur off her neck ... it was true beauty.'

On 1 October, he woke up, calmly grabbed a baseball bat from his room and beat his 50-year-old mother, Mary, breaking her jaw and smashing her skull. He chased her into her bedroom where he stabbed her to death with a butcher's knife. He then cleaned up the blood, washed his clothes and picked up his writings and a shotgun. At his trial he claimed to remember nothing of the killing.

He took his mother's Chevy Corsica and drove to Pearl High School. He met Sledge there and handed him the pages of writing. Sledge is said to have taken to his heels and hidden in the school's library as Woodham returned to the car for the shotgun. He walked into school, the rifle hidden beneath his blue trenchcoat, found Christina Menefee among a crowd of students and shot her dead at point-blank range. Then he shot and killed Menefee's best friend, Lydia Drew. He re-loaded and continued to fire into the crowd, ultimately wounding seven other students.

He ran back to his car and as he tried to drive away, another student blocked his exit. In the meantime, assistant principal Myrick had rushed to his truck to retrieve the .45 calibre pistol he kept there. He then stopped Woodham, who had run from his car and subdued him.

Luke Woodham was found to have been perfectly sane at the time of the killings, and was given three life sentences and 140 years for seven counts of aggravated assault. The charges against Grant Boyette and Justin Sledge, initially conspiracy to murder, were changed to accessory to murder. Boyette eventually pleaded guilty to the much lesser charge of preventing a principal from doing his job and was sentenced to a boot camp-style programme called Regimented Inmate Discipline, or RID, which lasts up to six months at Parchman Penitentiary, and five years supervized probation. He maintains his innocence.

The shootings at Pearl High School were the first of their kind and set a new and deadly 'fashion' among American high-school pupils for gunning down their fellow students.

BELOW: Mug shot of Pearl High School student Justin Sledge, aged 16, 7 October, 1997.

GARY HEIDNIK
3520 NORTH MARSHALL STREET,
PENNSYLVANIA, USA

3520 NORTH MARSHALL STREET LOOKED, TO MOST PEOPLE, LIKE ANY OTHER HOUSE IN THE AREA - DILAPIDATED AND SEEDY LOOKING, BUT APPARENTLY NORMAL. INSIDE THOUGH, GARY HEIDNIK'S HOME WAS ANYTHING BUT. HE KEPT YOUNG GIRLS SHACKLED IN THE CELLAR LIKE STRAY ANIMALS, THERE TO CATER FOR HIS EVERY SEXUAL NEED AND PROVIDE HIM WITH THE FAMILY HE SO CRAVED. WHEN THE GIRLS DIDN'T BEHAVE THEMSELVES, HE MURDERED, MUTILATED AND COOKED THEM UP IN HIS KITCHEN.

Josefina Rivera awoke to the full horror of her situation. She lay on a dirty mattress in the centre of a small room. Metal clamps circling her ankles were connected to a chain which was fastened around a large pipe fixed to the ceiling. He had brought her here the previous evening after she had had an argument with her boyfriend and stormed out of the house. As he had been showing her round the house, he had jumped her from behind and started to choke her. Then he had pushed her into this room and chained her up. The last she remembered was him going to sleep, his head on her lap.

His name was Gary Heidnik and he lived at 3520 North Marshall Street, in North Philadelphia. This was not the first time he had done this.

Heidnik had not been very successful at school and, in 1961, he joined the army, serving as a medic. However, his mental instability resulted in an honourable discharge after 14 months. 'Schizoid

personality disorder' was how they described his condition. He met a woman called Betty through a matrimonial service and, after writing to each other for two years, they married.

Heidnik's first brush with the law, in 1976, resulted from a rent dispute with a tenant of a house he owned. He fired a gun at the man, grazing his face with the bullet. Then, in 1978, he kept his girlfriend's cognitively disabled sister prisoner in a storage cupboard in the basement of his house. He had taken her out of the hospital in which she lived and, when she was eventually discovered, they found she had been raped and sodomized. He was arrested, charged with kidnapping, rape, unlawful restraint, false imprisonment, involuntary deviant sexual intercourse and interfering with the custody of a committed person, receiving a custodial sentence of three to seven years. The sentence was overturned on appeal, however, and he spent three years in mental institutions,

BELOW: Police search for evidence in Heidnik's basement, where his female captives were horrifically tortured and sexually abused.

instead of prison. He came out in 1983.

In 1986, his wife, Betty, left him for good. The marriage had been an unhappy one and he had raped and beat her. She was pregnant, however, and gave birth to his son after she left him. He would never see the boy.

She went to the police and Heidnik was arrested yet again, on charges of assault, indecent assault, spousal rape and involuntary deviant sexual intercourse. He was lucky, however. Betty failed to show at the preliminary hearing and the charges were dropped.

In 1986, Heidnik hatched a plan to kidnap ten women who would have his babies. The first was Josefina Rivera, who he picked up on 26 November and took home in his silver and white Cadillac Coup de Ville. She was impressed by his expensive jewellery and watch and by the 1971 Rolls-Royce parked in his driveway. But she was puzzled by the seedy, dilapidated nature of the house, the cheap, dirty clothes he wore and the strange key he used to open his door. He told her he had fashioned it so that a part of the key remained in the lock. No one else could get in without that key.

Now, the following morning, she took in the room she found herself in. In the middle of the floor, a pit had been excavated. Heidnik returned and began to make this hole wider and deeper. To her increasing horror, he told her of his plan. He then raped her for the first of many times. Later that morning she began to scream, hoping to alert neighbours or passers-by, but Heidnik came back and used a stick to viciously beat her. He then shoved her into the pit, covering it with wood and weighing it down.

Not long after, Heidnik removed the wood above her prison and helped her out of the pit. There was now another woman in the room, and Heidnik introduced her as Sandy Lindsay. He had befriended her at the Elwyn Institute, a local hospital for the mentally and physically handicapped. She had already had an abortion when she became pregnant with Heidnik's baby. When he had found out, he had been

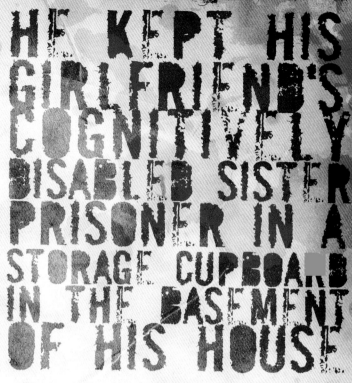

HE KEPT HIS GIRLFRIEND'S COGNITIVELY DISABLED SISTER PRISONER IN A STORAGE CUPBOARD IN THE BASEMENT OF HIS HOUSE

enraged and offered her $1000 (£500) to have his baby. She refused and he kidnapped her.

Sandy's family began looking for her, and he wrote a note to her mother, posting it in New York, explaining that she was going away for a while.

Josefina and Sandy remained in the room together for weeks, being fed only now and then and being raped on a regular basis. They were beaten when they screamed for help and were punished by a visit to the pit whenever they breached one of his rules. He would also suspend them, for hours at a time, by one arm.

Meanwhile, Sandy's mother told the police that she thought her daughter was being held against her will by a man she knew as Gary, and gave them Heidnik's address. When an officer went to the house, he got no reply and the case was dropped.

In late December, Heidnik brought another victim into the room, 19-year-old Lisa. He was just under a third of the way to his ten slaves. 23-year-old Deborah Dudley, arrived shortly after. She was feisty, often fought back and was savagely beaten.

Heidnik now began to use the girls against each other, appointing one to be in charge when he went out and to report any

infractions to him on his return. She would then be ordered to beat the others. If no one was reported to have misbehaved, he would beat them all, anyway.

Their food depended on his changeable moods. Eventually, he reduced them to a diet of tinned dog food, beating them until they ate it.

A fifth girl arrived in the middle of January – Jacqueline, a petite 18-year-old. She was so small, in fact, that the shackles would not fit, and he had to improvise with handcuffs. It was Josefina's birthday that day, and he surprised them with a meal of Chinese food. Josefina was rapidly turning into his favourite. He also thought – wrongly as it turned out – that she and Sandy were pregnant by him.

In early February, Sandy grew sick and, after a week, she died. He dragged her upstairs and, before too long, the surviving girls were horrified to hear the sound of a chain saw. They could only imagine what he was doing – when one of his dogs came into the room carrying a long, meaty bone, their worst fears were confirmed. Heidnik had ground up Sandy's flesh and began serving it to the girls mixed with dog food.

He cooked other parts of the body and kept some in his fridge.

When the house began to smell very badly, as a result of the rotting flesh, the neighbours complained. Heidnik, smooth as ever, told the police officer who called round, that he had merely overcooked a roast dinner.

He became increasingly paranoid that the girls were plotting against him. Therefore, to put an end to this, he hung them from a beam, took a screwdriver and gouged inside their ears in an attempt to deafen them. The pain was intense and their screams were muffled by gags he had stuffed in their mouths. He left his favourite, Josefina alone.

One day, when Deborah had been causing her usual share of trouble, he unchained her and took her upstairs. When she returned, she was uncharacteristically withdrawn. He had lifted the lid of a pot on his stove, she told the others, and inside was the head of Sandy Lindsay. He showed her Sandy's ribcage cooking in the oven and opened the fridge to show her an arm and other parts of her body. He warned her that this is what would happen to her if she persisted in causing trouble.

He introduced new punishments, electrocuting the girls with bare wires, all except Josefina, who now slept in his bed and spent time alone with him. One day, he ordered her to fill the pit with water and threw the girls in. He then touched Deborah with the exposed wire and she writhed in agony before collapsing into the water. She was dead. He wrapped her body up and put it in his freezer.

As the weeks passed, he began to soften slightly towards the girls, letting them watch TV and giving them mattresses, blankets and pillows. He also began to let Josefina accompany him on trips out of the house, on one of which they disposed of Deborah's body. On another, they found a slave to replace Deborah, a woman called Agnes. Josefina, however, was merely waiting for her chance.

On 24 March, four months after she had been captured, she persuaded him to let her visit her family, on condition that she would bring back another woman. Naturally, as soon as her boyfriend opened the door to the apartment they shared, she blurted out her story. He found it hard to believe, and so did the police when they arrived. When she showed them the manacle marks on her ankles, they began to believe her.

They arrested Heidnik at a petrol station and then went to 3520 North Marshall Street, where they discovered the full horror of what he had done. The girls were chained to a beam and clad in nothing more than flimsy blouses and socks. They found Agnes cowering in the pit. In the kitchen, they found an industrial food processor, recently used, and an oven dish containing a human rib. When an officer opened the fridge door, he was confronted by a human forearm lying on one of the shelves.

Heidnik turned out to be a wealthy man, with $550,000 (£225,000) in an investment account. But it proved little help to him when he was put on trial. He was found guilty on two counts of first-degree murder, five of rape, six of kidnapping, four of aggravated assault and one of involuntary

deviate sexual intercourse. He was sentenced to death and, as he had done throughout the trial, showed not an iota of emotion as the sentence was read out.

Eleven years later, on 6 July, 1999, at 10.29pm, Gary Heidnik was executed by legal injection. No one came forward to claim his body.

BELOW: Police and workers from Philadelphia's Water Department investigate the sewer lines running under 3520 North Marshall Street.

COLUMBINE MASSACRE

COLUMBINE HIGH SCHOOL, JEFFERSON COUNTY, COLARADO, USA

ON 20 APRIL 1999, TWO BITTER AND ANGRY YOUNG MEN IN TRENCHCOATS OPENED FIRE ON THEIR CLASS MATES - JOKING FLIPPANTLY THAT THEY WERE 'JUST KILLING PEOPLE'. UNTIL THAT DAY, COLUMBINE HIGH SCHOOL HAD BEEN JUST LIKE ANY OTHER, DOMINATED BY THE SAME TEENAGE MINI-DRAMAS, BUT THEN THE CARNAGE BEGAN, AND GOING TO SCHOOL CHANGED FOREVER.

The signs had been there for all to see. 18-year-old Eric Harris's website, originally created to host new levels for the computer game Doom, created with the help of his friend, Dylan Klebold, 17, featured a blog which began to detail how to make bombs. The blog, launched in early 1997, discussed Harris's thoughts about parents, teachers and school friends. It demonstrated, to anyone reading it, just how much he was growing to hate the society in which he lived.

Few people visited the site, of course, but it was brought to the notice of the authorities when it ran death threats aimed at a Columbine pupil, Brooks Brown, as well as violent messages about students and teachers at the school. Jefferson County sheriff's office investigator, Michael Guerra drafted an affidavit to search Harris's home for explosives, but it was never executed.

Harris and Klebold had already been in trouble for stealing tools. Their sentence was attendance at various classes and regular meetings with parole officers. Harris was also seeing a psychologist, continuing to do so until shortly before the massacre. He had been put on a course

BELOW: The perpetrators of the Columbine High School massacre allegedly belonged to the Trench Coat Mafia.

of anti-depressants, including the drug Luvox, the side effects of which included increased aggression, loss of remorse, depersonalization and mania. With hindsight, this drug was not, perhaps, the best treatment for a young man at war with society.

As their murderous ambitions began to escalate, the two boys began to write journals in which they wrote about beating the death toll of the 1995 Oklahoma City bombing. Ideas included hijacking a plane and crashing it into a building in New York City, but eventually they settled on a plot to massacre as many of their classmates and teachers as they could.

The plan was to set off a couple of bombs in the school cafeteria and then shoot students as they fled. They would then enter the school and shoot as many as they could. The attack would progress to people living in houses adjacent to the school.

On the morning of Tuesday 20 April 1999 – Adolf Hitler's birthday and one day after the anniversaries of Oklahoma City and the deaths of David Koresh's Branch Davidians in the 51-day siege at Waco – the boys

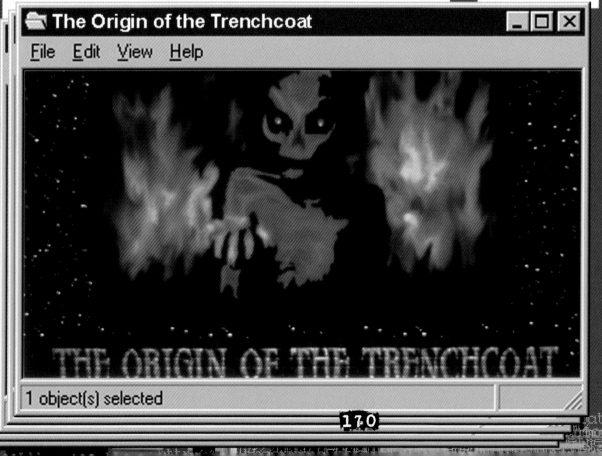

The Origin of the Trenchcoat

File   Edit   View   Help

THE ORIGIN OF THE TRENCHCOAT

1 object(s) selected

Rescuing Victim.jpg

File Edit View Help

1 object(s) selected

made a video in which they said farewell to friends and families and apologized for what they were about to do. They loaded up explosive devices they had constructed and the arsenal of weapons they had acquired in the previous few months – two 9mm firearms and a couple of 12-gauge shotguns. They then climbed into their cars and drove separately to Columbine High School.

Arriving at the school at 11.10am, they parked in separate car parks. En route, they had stopped to set up a small incendiary device in a field about 0.8km (0.5 miles) from the school. It partially exploded at 11.14am and is thought to have been intended as a diversion to keep emergency personnel busy.

Harris and Klebold, wearing trenchcoats, met up and armed a couple of large propane bombs before carrying them in duffel bags into the cafeteria. These were set to explode at 11.17am, destroying the café and bringing the library located above it crashing down. However, as the two boys waited by their cars for the explosions,

nothing happened, and it became obvious the bombs were duds.

Around this time, Brooks Brown, the boy Harris had threatened on his website, approached them; he and Harris had recently settled their differences. He asked them why they had missed a test earlier that morning, but Harris calmly told him it would be best if he went home. The tone of his voice suggested to Brown that something was seriously wrong and he did, indeed, set off for home.

As the bombs failed to detonate, the boys changed their plans, climbing, fully armed and carrying duffel bags filled with ammunition, to the top of the school's west entrance steps. It was now 11.19am and they had a view of the side entrance to the cafeteria, the school's main west entrance and the athletic fields. Harris yelled: 'Go! Go!' and the carnage began.

The first victims were Rachel Scott and Richard Castaldo, seated on the grass to the left of Harris and Klebold, enjoying lunch. Scott, hit four times, died instantly and Castaldo, hit eight times, was seriously

ABOVE: Armed police rescue unnamed victim from Columbine High School.

Peek -a- boo!

Klebold now began to make their way to the West Entrance, throwing pipe bombs as they went.

Teacher Patti Nielson was on her way outside to find out what the noise was, but was shot and hit in the shoulder by shrapnel and ran back inside, heading for the library where she ordered the students there to hide beneath the desks. She also called the police.

At 11.24am, a sheriff arrived and began firing at Harris and Klebold, who returned fire. He called in for back-up.

The two boys entered the school, shooting Stephanie Munson in the ankle in the North Hallway, before heading for the library. Coach William Sanders met them en route and was shot in the chest. He struggled into a science classroom where students tried to staunch the flow of blood. They put a sign in the classroom window, saying '1 bleeding to death'. Sanders died a few hours later.

Harris and Klebold threw bombs into the cafeteria as they approached the library. This time they exploded. At 11.29am, they entered the library where 52 students, two teachers and two librarians were hiding. Harris screamed at everyone to get up, but when no one did, he changed his order to, 'Everyone with a white cap or baseball cap, stand up!' meaning the school athletes. Again no one stood, and Harris shouted 'Fine, I'll start anyway!'

The massacre in the library was horrific in the extreme, as the two wandered round firing randomly or leaning down to look

wounded. It is reported that, as well as targeting the school's 'jocks' – athletes who wore white caps to mark their status at the school – who, according to some theories, had been bullying Harris and Klebold and making homophobic remarks about them, they also wanted to target Christians. To this end, it is reported that the killers first asked Rachel Scott if she believed in God and when she innocently replied, 'Yes I do', they opened fire on her.

Harris now pulled out his semi-automatic and shot Daniel Rohrbough and two friends, Sean Graves and Lance Kirklin, who had been standing on the west staircase, wounding all three. They then shot at pupils seated on the grass next to the steps, hitting Michael Johnson on the face, arms and leg. Johnson escaped and Mark Taylor, hit in the chest, arms and leg, collapsed to the ground pretending to be dead. Klebold walked down the steps, pausing to shoot the wounded Lance Kirklin in the face. Daniel Rohrbough was shot again, in the back, and died. Anne-Marie Hochhalter was wounded in the chest, arm, abdomen, back and left leg as she tried to get away at the entrance to the cafeteria. Harris and at the terrified students huddled together under desks before shooting them. At one point, Harris banged a desktop twice with his hand and then leant down to see Cassie Bernall cowering in terror. 'Peek-a-boo!', he sneered, before shooting her in the head. Unfortunately for him, the recoil of the gun sent it back hard into his face, breaking his nose.

In all, ten students died in the library and a further 12 were wounded.

Passing the library windows, they fired at police outside who were working to evacuate teachers and students. The officers returned fire.

At 11.37am, as they re-loaded their weapons, Klebold spoke to a student he knew, John Savage. When Savage asked Klebold what they were doing, he replied nonchalantly, 'Oh, just killing people.' He then allowed the boy to leave the library.

The two killers were now heard to remark how the novelty of shooting people had worn off. Klebold suggested it might be more fun to knife their victims. They then left the carnage of the library. It was 11.42am.

They wandered the corridors, firing randomly, and entered the cafeteria again, shooting at the propane bomb, trying, unsuccessfully, to detonate it. They threw a pipe bomb, which exploded, and headed back up the stairs. Passing a number of classrooms, they stared in the windows at the students cowering inside, but did not enter.

At 12.02pm, they went back into the library, now empty of all but the dead students. They shot at the police outside again and then, at 12.08pm, they turned their weapons on themselves. Eric Harris shot himself with a single shot in the mouth and Dylan Klebold shot himself in the head.

Going to school in America would never be the same again.

BELOW: Columbine shooters Eric Harris, left, and Dylan Klebold appear on a surveillance tape in the cafeteria at Columbine High School.

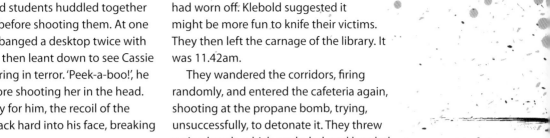

IAN
HUNTLEY

5 COLLEGE CLOSE,
SOHAM, CAMBRIDGESHIRE, ENGLAND

THE HUNT FOR HOLLY WELLS AND
JESSICA CHAPMAN WAS ONE OF THE
MOST HIGHLY PUBLICIZED MISSING
PERSON SEARCHES IN BRITISH HISTORY.
THE WHOLE NATION GRIEVED WHEN,
ON 17 AUGUST, 2002, THE REMAINS OF
THE TWO GIRLS WERE FINALLY FOUND.
SIGNALS FROM JESSICA'S MOBILE PHONE
WERE TRACED TO AN AREA NEAR TO 5
COLLEGE CLOSE - THE HOME OF A MAN
WHO HAS SINCE BECOME INFAMOUS -
IAN HUNTLEY - CHILD KILLER.

Sunday 4 August, 2002, was a hot and sunny day in East Cambridgeshire and the people of the small town of Soham were out in their gardens enjoying the bright sunshine. The Wells family had invited some family and friends over to their house for a barbecue and everyone was having a lovely time. Holly Wells and Jessica Chapman, both aged ten, were proudly wearing new red Manchester United strips, the name of their hero, David Beckham, emblazoned on the back. They posed together for a photograph before eating. It would be the last photograph of the two little girls alive.

After dinner, Holly and Jessica asked if they could go out and buy sweets at the Soham Sports Centre, not far from the Wells house. When they failed to return and their increasingly frantic parents were unable to obtain a reply from Jessica's mobile phone, which they knew she had taken with her, they reported the girls missing and, around midnight, a police search of the area was launched.

The search continued the next day and was joined by hundreds of local people. Posters were issued carrying pictures of the girls in the hope that someone's memory would be jogged and some vital piece of information would lead to their discovery. David Beckham, whose name was on the shirts they were wearing, made an appeal on television for their safe return. But still there was no sign of them and, as time passed, hopes of finding them alive began to fade.

Among the witnesses who had been the last to see Holly and Jessica on the Sunday night was 29-year-old Ian Huntley, caretaker at the girls' primary school, Soham Village College. He claimed to have seen them shortly after they had left the barbecue, walking past 5 College Close, the house he shared with his fiancée, Maxine Carr, a teaching assistant at the school.

Huntley's house and the school where he worked were searched, in order to eliminate him as a suspect, and, although nothing was found to link him with the girls' disappearance, police still retained some suspicions about him. He asked too many questions and seemed to be taking an unhealthy interest in the case. He was even interviewed on television about it.

When, a week later, investigators returned to Soham College for a further search, they made a harrowing find – the partially burned Manchester United shirts the girls had been wearing that afternoon, and their shoes, hidden in a rubbish bin.

Huntley and Maxine Carr were arrested immediately on suspicion of murder.

The following day, 17 August, a game warden, walking near the RAF Lakenheath airbase in Suffolk made a tragic discovery, the partially burned remains of Holly and Jessica. They had died of asphyxiation before being burned.

BELOW: A police handout photograph shows murdered Cambridgeshire schoolgirls Holly Wells, left and Jessica Chapman, in the Manchester United football club shirts they were wearing on August 4, 2002, when they were last seen alive.

The nation was shocked and the evidence against Huntley began to build. To begin with, he was familiar with the area in which the girls were found, as he used to go plane-spotting there. It was also not far from where his father lived.

The forensic evidence was even more damning. Fibres from his clothes, the carpets in 5 College Close and from his car were found on the girls' shirts. His hair was also found on them. The last signal from Jessica's mobile was traced to a location close to his house.

On 20 August, Ian Huntley was formally charged with the murders of Holly Wells and Jessica Chapman and Maxine Carr was charged with assisting an offender as well as conspiring to pervert the course of justice. She had provided him with an alibi, claiming that she had been in the house with him on the Sunday evening when, she had, in fact, been hundreds of miles away in Grimsby, visiting her mother, as phone records confirmed.

The evidence presented at the trial of Huntley and Carr was overwhelming. His fingerprints were found on the bag in which the girls' clothing had been disposed of. Huntley had been seen meticulously cleaning his red Ford Fiesta the day after the girls' disappearance, replacing the flooring in the boot with a piece of carpet. He had changed all four tyres and tried to bribe the mechanic who carried out the work to put down a false number plate on the paperwork.

Several weeks into the trial, however, Huntley made an astonishing confession.

He admitted being responsible for the girls' deaths, but claimed that it had all been an accident. He said that they had come to his door to talk to Carr, but that Holly had a nosebleed. Taking them into the bathroom to clean Holly up, he had accidentally pushed her into the bath that was half full of water. At that point, he claimed, Jessica began to scream and, in a panic, he put his hand over her mouth to quieten her, but had suffocated her 'accidentally'. He said he then turned round to Holly in the bath only to find that she was also dead.

He had put the girls into the back of his car and drove to Lakenheath where he removed their clothing, poured petrol over them and set fire to them.

Carr added her own confession a few days later. She said she had provided him with an alibi because she wanted to protect him. She knew that he had been accused of rape in 1998, but the case had been dropped due to lack of evidence. But, she knew he would lose his job if the case came to light. She also did not believe him capable of murder.

On 17 December, the jury found Huntley guilty of the murder of the two girls. He was given to two life sentences, while Maxine Carr was found guilty of conspiring to pervert the course of justice and went to prison for three and a half years.

BELOW: This undated handout photo shows the bathroom at 5 College Close, where Ian Huntley claims the girls died accidently.

ROBERT PICKTON
PICKTON PIG FARM,
953 DOMINION AVENUE,
VANCOUVER, CANADA

TODAY, THE INFAMOUS PICKTON FARM,
AT 953 DOMINION AVE, PORT COQUILAM,
IS AVAILABLE FOR REDEVELOPMENT.
AT LEAST 40 SINGLE FAMILY LOTS AND
NEARLY 190 TOWNHOUSES COULD
SOON BE BUILT ON THIS SITE, BUT,
BECAUSE OF THE NOTORIETY OF THIS
MUDDY PATCH OF SCRUBLAND, IT IS
UNLIKELY THAT IT WILL BE PICKED UP BY
PROPERTY DEVELOPERS AT ANYTHING
MORE THAN A BARGAIN-BASEMENT
PRICE. IN 2002, THIS HUMBLE PIG FARM,
ON THE OUTSKIRTS OF VANCOUVER,
SUDDENLY FOUND ITSELF SLAP-BANG
AT THE CENTRE OF THE BIGGEST, MOST
EXPENSIVE MURDER INVESTIGATION IN
CANADIAN HISTORY. ITS OWNER, ROBERT
WILLIAM PICKTON, WAS CHARGED WITH
MURDERING SCORES OF VANCOUVER
PROSTITUTES AND FEEDING THEIR
DISMEMBERED BODIES TO HIS
BELOVED PIGS.

The Downtown Eastside neighbourhood of Vancouver, an area of ten blocks between the Pacific Central Station and Vancouver Harbour, is one of the poorest and most deprived parts of Canada. Since the early 1980s, it has had the highest rate of drug addiction and HIV infection in the country. In recent years, the area has attracted a wider social mix, leading some long-term residents to complain that it is becoming gentrified, but it still remains the hang-out of petty criminals and drug addicts, along with the dispossessed and destitute. The low-rent hotels along Main Street and Hastings Street are well known, locally, as premises where prostitutes live and work. A high proportion of them come from Canada's aboriginal communities, and almost all have been forced into selling their bodies because of poverty or to pay for their drug habits. Over a period of 20 years, from the early 1980s to 2002, it was also the neighbourhood from where more than 60 women went missing. The majority of the missing women have not been heard from since.

On 23 June 1983, 23 year-old Rebecca Guno was reported missing. She was a sex-trade worker and drug addict from the Low Track, as the Downtown Eastside is known to the women who work there. Most people assumed that she had simply moved on

BELOW: An undated aerial photo of the Pickton farm, taken by the Royal Canadian Mounted Police during their investigation of accused serial killer Robert Pickton.

to ply her trade elsewhere, or decided to leave the profession in order to make a new start. Sex-trade workers are notoriously difficult to trace for obvious reasons, many do not have employment records, bank accounts or permanent addresses. Years later, Rebecca Guno would become the first on the list of women missing from the Low Track compiled by a community organisation in an attempt to attract police and media attention to the case. For 15 years the police had received regular reports of missing women, sometimes within days of the disappearance and sometimes months or even years later, but many Low Track-residents believed that the police had done little about the disappearances other than to add each name to the register of missing persons.

By September 1998, there were more than 20 prostitutes missing from the Downtown Eastside. The Missing Women Task Force was set-up, comprising detectives from the Vancouver Police Department and the Royal Canadian Mounted Police. The investigation initially focused on known sex offenders. There were plenty of candidates along the Pacific north-west coast. Among the suspects was the then unidentified Green River Killer, who murdered 49 prostitutes in Seattle in the early 1980s. Gary Ridgway was unmasked as the culprit for the Seattle killings in 2001, and was known to have visited Vancouver, but, even if he continued to kill while he was there, he could not have been responsible for all the disappearances from the Low Track.

Shortly after the task force was set up in 1998, 37-year-old Bill Hiscox contacted them regarding two brothers he worked for in the vehicle salvage business. Robert Pickton, generally known as Willy, and his younger brother, David, lived in Port Coquitlam, a town on the eastern edge of Vancouver that was gradually being swallowed up by the expanding city. The brothers were pig farmers and had sold off most of their land to property developers. They retained about 5.5 hectares (14 acres), where they continued to keep pigs. Bill Hiscox was introduced to the brothers by a helpful relative, a girlfriend of Willy's, at a difficult time in his life. When Bill began working at the farm he suffered from drink and drug addictions which, the defence later claimed, effected his credibility as a witness for the prosecution. The Pickton brothers ran a salvage business on the farm, which became littered with broken-down old cars. Robert Pickton later claimed that these vehicles were the source of much of the evidence against him. The Pickton brothers also ran a registered charity, called the Piggy Palace Good Times Society. Despite its charitable status, it is widely believed that they used the society to organize wild parties, which they held in a converted barn on the edge of the farm, called the Piggy Palace. The prosecution alleged that the entertainment at these parties was provided by an ever-changing cast of sex-trade workers from the Low Track.

Bill Hiscox read the newspaper reports about the increasing number of prostitutes who had gone missing. He informed that police he had seen plenty of women's possessions, including purses and IDs, in a mobile home on the pig farm when he had gone there to pick up his wages. Robert Pickton didn't usually say much, but, according to Hiscox, when he did talk he bragged about picking up prostitutes in the

Downtown Eastside, where he was a well-known figure. It was not hard for Hiscox to make the connection between Pickton and the missing women. The police were well acquainted with both of the Pickton brothers. David had been in trouble with the police a number of times, including, in 1992, when he received a $,1000 (£500) fine for sexual assault. Robert was arrested in 1997 after Wendy Eistetter, a Low Track prostitute, alleged he had attacked her with a knife at one of the Piggy Palace parties, stabbing her three times before she managed to escape. The investigation was dropped in 1998. It is important to note that no charges were ever brought against Robert Pickton in relation to the incident. However, when Hiscox went to the police with his suspicions, they took them seriously enough to search the farm on three separate occasions. Although they found nothing incriminating, both brothers were considered to be 'persons of interest' in the continuing investigation.

Prostitutes continued to go missing from the Low Track throughout 1999 and 2000. The number of reports coming in were increasing, making it impossible for the police to continue the low-key approach to the investigation they had adopted. In 2001, with almost 60 women missing, the task force finally announced to the public that they were looking for a serial killer. The increased publicity the announcement generated brought several women forward who had been on the missing list, but prostitutes were still vanishing from the Low Track. In August 2001, 29-year-old Sereena Abotsway, who was one of the women involved with the protests to the police over their perceived inaction, disappeared from the Downtown Eastside. Although she had been working as a prostitute for ten years, she maintained regular contact with her adopted family, who were worried when they didn't hear from her on her 30th birthday on 20 August. Three months later Mona Wilson, 26, went missing. The police were informed on 30 November, a week after she had last been seen.

Early in 2002, a man who knew both of the Pickton brothers informed the Vancouver police that there were illegal firearms being kept on their pig farm. It gave the police sufficient cause to obtain a warrant to search the farm again. Several unlicensed firearms were recovered and Robert Pickton, who was 52 at the time, was taken into custody. The search didn't stop there. Human remains, and some possessions belonging to Sereena Abotsway and Mona Wilson, were also found on the farm. DNA analysis of extensive bloodstains on a mattress in the mobile home on the farm connected them to Mona Wilson. Robert Pickton was granted bail on the firearms charges, but, on 22 February 2002, he was arrested again, this time for the first-degree murder of Sereena Abotsway and Mona Wilson.

After the discovery of human remains, the entire farm was cordoned off and an extensive search began. More than 100 forensic scientists were involved and two huge soil sifters were employed to go through the soil over the whole area of the farm. Body parts of some of the missing women were found in waste bins in the slaughterhouse on the farm. Human bones were also found in the pig pens, leading to suspicions that bodies were butchered, rendered and fed to the pigs. Some of the human remains are also thought to have been mixed with pork and given out for human consumption.

The investigation progressed slowly. The remains and DNA samples of 30 different women were found on the farm altogether. Most of the women were on the list of the missing prostitutes, but three remain unidentified. At preliminary hearings, beginning in January 2006, Robert Pickton was charged with 27 counts of murder.

BELOW: Investigators dig and test samples from one of many mounds of soil at the Pickton pig farm in Port Coquitlam, British Columbia, 5 April, 2002.

One count was dismissed through lack of evidence, and the judge decided to split the trial into two sections, to reduce the burden on the jury. The first trial, which began on 22 January 2007, concerned six counts of murder, including those of Sereena Abotsway and Mona Wilson. The other alleged victims were Marnie Frey, Andrea Joesbury, Georgina Papin and Brenda Wolfe, all of whom disappeared from 1999 to 2001.

A reporting embargo imposed by the trial judge prevented most of the details of the evidence against Pickton leaking out before it had been presented to the jury. On the first day of the trial, the prosecution outlined how an undercover police officer, posing as a man charged with attempted murder, shared a cell with Pickton. They discussed the case and Pickton even talked on video, saying he had killed 49 women before he was caught and was disappointed because he had wanted to make it an even 50. Pickton told the police officer he was caught because he had got 'sloppy', failing to clean up after killing four of the women. During the same, filmed conversation, Pickton said that his plan was 'to let everything die for a while (before) doing 25 new ones'. The jury also saw Pickton saying that he would be 'bigger' than the Green River Killer, seconds later he turns directly to the camera in the cell and waves saying 'hello'.

Pickton officially denied any involvement with the missing women, pleading 'not guilty' to all charges. Throughout the trial he remained passive, staring blankly out at the court, as if bored by the proceedings.

A number of witnesses described Pickton as being of below average intelligence and under the control of his younger brother. Others have given details of conversations they had with Pickton in which he outlined his preferred methods of killing. He apparently explained to one acquaintance how he injected drug addicts using a syringe containing a solution of windscreen cleaner. To another, Pickton is thought to have said he liked to handcuff prostitutes to a bed before strangling them and then feeding their ground-up bodies to the pigs.

One of the main questions arising during the trial has been whether Robert Pickton acted alone or if other people were also involved. A man who butchered pigs in the slaughterhouse on the farm has been questioned about what, exactly, he was cutting up, but no charges have been brought against him.

There is also intense speculation concerning how much, if anything, David Pickton knew about the killings. Robert Pickton has so far been found guilty of the first six murders. The second trial is set to continue and, no doubt, there is a great deal more evidence to be heard. With the police still investigating Robert Pickton's association with many more women on the missing persons list, it could be many years before the full story emerges.

ABOVE: Police released these photos on 19 September 2002, featuring four women whose remains were found at the Pickton farm. They are Helen Hallmark, Jennifer Furminger, Georgia Papin and Patricia Johnson.

VIRGINIA TECH MASSACRE

VIRGINIA TECH UNIVERSITY, VIRGINIA, USA

VIRGINIA TECH WAS FOUNDED IN 1872 AS VIRGINIA AGRICULTURAL AND MECHANICAL COLLEGE. ITS MOTTO IS UT PROSIM, WHICH TRANSLATES AS 'THAT I MAY SERVE'. THE ONLY THING PUPIL, SEUNG-HUI CHO NEEDED SERVING WITH WAS A COMPULSORY COMMITMENT-ORDER UNDER VIRGINIA'S MENTAL HEALTH LEGISLATION, BUT UNFORTUNATELY THAT NEVER HAPPENED. CONSEQUENTLY HE WAS ABLE TO COMMIT THE BLOODIEST SCHOOL SHOOTING IN AMERICA'S HISTORY.

Virginia Tech

1872

Welcome Visitors: Please obtain your required Parking Permit at the Visitor Information Center on Southgate Drive

Seung-Hui Cho had always been an odd, strangely menacing character, even when very young. His family had long worried about him, some family members suspecting that he possibly suffered from autism. He spoke rarely and mumbled when he did. As a result, he became a victim of bullying and retreated even further into himself. Eventually, he was diagnosed with depression and selective mutism, a social anxiety disorder that prevented him from speaking. He received some therapy, but discontinued it.

When he went to Virginia Tech to study English, in 2003, his behaviour became even more erratic. He was obviously intelligent, but was an insecure loner who appeared arrogant and never removed his sunglasses, even indoors. Having taught him for only six weeks, poetry teacher Nikki Giovanni, had him removed from her class in autumn 2005, after he had photographed female students' legs under their desks and because of the violent, obscene poems he had been writing. Giovanni communicated her concerns to her department head, Lucinda Roy, who passed them to the student affairs office and the dean's office, but, as he had made no overt threats against anyone, there was nothing they could do.

Roy made efforts to help the boy, working one-to-one with him, but became concerned with her own personal safety, to the extent that she invented a code to pass to a colleague if she felt threatened. She urged Cho to seek counselling, but he never did.

Meanwhile, Cho's previous mental health problems were not divulged due to privacy laws.

When he arrived at Virginia Tech, Cho had found it difficult to talk to anyone, even failing to respond to greetings when he passed other students. On the class sign-in sheet, on which pupils had to write their names, he wrote only a question mark, and it was as 'Question Mark' that he often introduced himself to people. He became known as 'The Question Mark Kid'.

He never seemed to do any work, attend classes or read books. A room-mate reported that he sat on a wooden rocking chair by a window staring out at the lawn for hours on end. He typed endlessly on his laptop and was once spotted riding his bike in endless circles around the dormitory car park. He was obsessed by the song Shine by rock band, Collective Soul, playing it continuously. Andy Koch, another room-mate, reported receiving repeated mobile phone calls from Cho in which he called himself 'Question Mark' and claimed to be Koch's brother. He informed Koch that he had an imaginary girlfriend called Jelly, a supermodel who lived in outer space, travelled by spaceship and knew Cho by the pet name, Spanky. On another occasion, during a holiday break, Cho called Koch and claimed to be holidaying with Russian president, Vladimir Putin. His behaviour was becoming so bizarre that Koch and other room-mates advised female students not to visit them in their room.

These concerns were exacerbated by the fact that he had been accused on several occasions of stalking female students, sending them unsolicited text messages and writing lines of Shakespeare on their

doors. After his final stalking of a female student had met with no response from her, he texted Koch, 'I might as well kill myself now'. Koch, worried for Cho's safety, alerted the authorities.

On 13 December 2005, Cho was declared to be 'mentally ill and in need of hospitalization' and was temporarily detained at Carilion St Albans Behavioral Health Center in Christiansburg, Virginia, pending a commitment hearing before the Montgomery County, Virginia district court. However, the recommendation was simply that he undergo outpatient treatment for his condition and he was released. Critically, because he had not been involuntarily committed to a mental health facility, he could still legally purchase firearms under Virginia law.

He purchased two guns – a .22-caliber Walther P22 semi-automatic handgun and, a month later, a 9mm semi-automatic Glock 19 handgun. Virginia law prohibited the purchase of two guns within a period of 30 days. On the morning of 16 April, he was ready to emulate his heroes, Dylan Klebold and Eric Harris, the perpetrators of the Columbine High School massacre in 1999, an event that had thrilled him.

OPPOSITE PAGE: A US flag flys at half-mast outside Burrus Hall on the campus of Virginia Tech in Blacksburg, Virginia, where 33 people were shot and killed on 17 April 2007.

That morning, at around 7am, Cho gained access to West Ambler Johnston hall, a residential hall at Virginia Tech that housed 894 students. It is not known how he got in there at that time as he had a pass card that only allowed him entry after 7.30 am. He proceeded to the room of a 19-year-old freshman student, Emily J Hilscher, and shot her and a senior, Ryan C Clark, dead. He then returned to his own room where he cleaned himself up, before deleting all his email correspondence and removing the hard drive from his computer. An hour later, he was seen in the vicinity of a duck pond on the campus into which, it is believed, he might have thrown the hard drive and his mobile phone. However, no trace of either has ever been found.

Meanwhile, emergency services were responding to the earlier incident. Critically, however, in decisions that were later heavily criticized, the campus authorities and police did not order a lockdown of the university buildings. Neither did they cancel that morning's classes until the shooter was caught.

Carrying a backpack in which were chains, locks, a hammer, a knife, his two guns and almost 400 rounds of ammunition, Cho next visited the local post office, where he posted a package containing his writings and some video recordings of himself to NBC News. These would arrive at the television station the following day.

Shortly after, he arrived at Norris Hall where Engineering Science and Mechanics were taught. Inside, he chained the main doors shut, taping a message to them that a bomb would be detonated if they were tampered with. He then headed for

BELOW: A still from footage that NBC News received from Cho Seung-Hui, the Virginia Tech shooter.

There were 13 students in the room and after Cho had shot dead the professor he opened fire on the terrified students, killing nine of them and wounding two the second floor of the building where a number of classrooms were situated.

He is said to have looked into a couple of classrooms before launching his first attack. It was an Advanced Hydrology class, taught by Professor GV Loganathan in Room 206. There were 13 students in the room and after Cho had shot dead the professor he opened fire on the terrified students, killing nine of them and wounding two.

Across the corridor, in Room 207, Christopher Bishop was teaching a German class. Cho entered the room and opened fire, killing Bishop and four more students. In Rooms 204 and 211, he continued his spree, shooting more students and teachers. He went back to some of the classrooms more than once, firing, in total, more than 174 rounds. In other classrooms, as soon as the gunfire was heard, students and teachers barricaded doors with whatever they could find.

In Room 204, Mathematics and Engineering professor and Holocaust survivor, Liviu Libresco succeeded in holding the classroom door until most of his panicked students had escaped via the windows, but Cho fired through the door killing him.

In a French class, in Room 211, teacher Jocelyne Couture-Nowak similarly attempted to block the door, ordering her students to the rear of the class. Again, she was shot through the door. A student, Henry Lee, who had tried to help her, was also killed.

When Cho was seen heading towards Room 205, a student, Zach Petkewicz, pushed a large table up against the door. After failing to gain entry and shooting several rounds through the door, Cho moved on.

Meanwhile, in Room 207, where Cho had already shot a number of people, some students barricaded the door and tended to the wounded, preventing him from re-entering the room.

By this time, 30 people, students and teachers were dead and 17 were wounded.

Outside, the police were trying to get into the building but were being prevented from doing so by the chains with which Cho had locked them. One officer succeeded in shooting off a deadbolt on a laboratory door and they entered the building. As they made for the second floor, they heard Cho's last shot. When they found him, he had a single, self-inflicted bullet wound to the temple.

He had more than emulated the Columbine killers. The Virginia Tech massacre became the deadliest school shooting in American history.

INDEX